The Salad Bar

The Salad Bar

Sara Lewis

LOVE FOOD™

This edition published by Parragon Books Ltd in 2014

LOVE FOOD is an imprint of Parragon Books Ltd

Parragon Books Ltd
Chartist House, 15–17 Trim Street
Bath, BA1 1HA, UK

www.parragon.com/lovefood

ISBN: 978-1-4723-4100-6

Printed in China

Created and produced by Pene Parker and Becca Spry
New recipes and food styling: Sara Lewis
Photographer: Haraala Hamilton

Notes for the reader
This book uses both metric and imperial measurements. Follow the
same units of measurement throughout: do not mix metric and
imperial. All spoon measurements are level: teaspoons are assumed
to be 5 ml and tablespoons are assumed to be 15 ml. Unless otherwise
stated, milk is assumed to be skimmed, eggs and individual
vegetables are medium, pepper is freshly ground black pepper and all
root vegetables should be peeled prior to use. Garnishes, decorations
and serving suggestions are all optional and not necessarily included
in the recipe ingredients or method. Any optional ingredients and
seasoning to taste are not included in the nutritional analysis.
While the author has made all reasonable efforts to ensure that the
information contained in this book is accurate and up to date at
the time of publication, anyone reading this book should note the
following important points:-

• Medical and pharmaceutical knowledge is constantly changing
and the author and the publisher cannot and do not guarantee the
accuracy or appropriateness of the contents of this book;

• In any event, this book is not intended to be, and should not be relied
upon, as a substitute for appropriate, tailored professional advice.
Both the author and the publisher strongly recommend that a doctor
or other healthcare professional is consulted before embarking on
major dietary changes;

• For the reasons set out above, and to the fullest extent permitted
by law, the author and the publisher: (i) cannot and do not accept
any legal duty of care or responsibility in relation to the accuracy or
appropriateness of the contents of this book, even where expressed
as "advice" or using other words to this effect; and (ii) disclaim any
liability, loss, damage or risk that may be claimed or incurred as a
consequence - directly or indirectly - of the use and/or application of
any of the contents of this book.

The salad bar

Salads have come a long way from the simple lettuce, tomato and cucumber-based meals our mothers used to serve. Foreign holidays have inspired a passion for culinary exploration, and with so many exciting ingredients now available in the shops, we can recreate salads from all over the world and experiment with new ideas.

Salads combine a variety of textures, with delicate lettuce leaves contrasting, for instance, with crunchy celery, radishes, seeds and nuts, and creamy avocado or Brie. Often salads mix up tastes too, with salty feta cheese sharing a plate with peppery rocket leaves, or bitter radicchio flavoured with sweet aged balsamic vinegar.

The key to a healthy diet

Nutritionists agree that the key to a healthy diet is variety. Eating more vegetables and fruit can help you look good and feel great and give you lots of energy. It can also help to prevent some cancers and lower the risk of coronary heart disease, diabetes and certain digestive problems.

It is recommended that we should aim to eat at least five portions of vegetables and fruit each day and reduce our consumption of meat, fat and sugary foods. Eating more salads is an excellent way to achieve this.

Most ingredients in a salad are served raw or lightly cooked, which means the nutrient levels are at their optimum. Raw foods tend to need more chewing than cooked foods, and take longer for the body to digest, leaving you feeling fuller for longer, so you are less likely to over-eat.

Salads aren't just for summer. By using seasonal ingredients such as asparagus in late spring, lettuces in summer, squashes in autumn, and root vegetables, kale, grains and pulses in winter, you can enjoy a healthy diet all year round.

Salads don't have to be cold either; they can include warm grains, roasted vegetables, strips of seared steak or stir-fried prawns, for example. In colder months, add heat to dressings with spices, grated fresh ginger and garlic.

Preparing salad leaves

Leaves are delicate and can bruise easily. They need washing; even bags of ready-washed salads benefit from a rinse as they tend to have been washed with chlorine-like chemicals when packaged. Separate leaves, then put them in a sink of cold water, turn them to loosen and remove any dirt, then drain in a colander. Pat dry with a clean tea-towel or dry in a salad spinner. Any unused leaves can be packed into a plastic box or bag, sealed and stored in the vegetable compartment in the bottom of the fridge. Add dressings at the last minute so the leaves don't wilt.

Lettuce who's who

A huge range of salad leaves is sold in the shops. But why not grow your own? Rocket, baby chard and mizuna are all easy to grow in a small flower bed, plant pot or window box, and the first leaves can be harvested within six weeks of planting.

Butterhead or basic round lettuce — soft, round lettuce with a pale-green heart. It doesn't keep well, so use on the day of purchase.

Chard leaves — tiny red-veined green leaves with red stems. Ruby chard has deep red leaves and stems. Also try small newly shooting leaves of Swiss chard or beetroot.

Chicory — pale, compact, spear-shaped leaves with pale green or red tips and a crisp, bitter flavour.

Cos and Romaine lettuce — long, thin lettuces with dark green outer leaves that change to pale green at the heart. They are famously used to make the classic Caesar salad.

Dandelion — not so readily available from shops, but young dark leaves can be picked from the garden, although they must be washed well before being eaten. Longer, yellow, thin-stemmed French dandelions (or *pissenlit*) can be bought from specialist greengrocers.

Frisée — sometimes called curly endive, frisée lettuce is a member of the chicory family. The spreading frond-like leaves taste a little bitter. It can be made into a salad on its own or mixed with other leaves.

Iceberg — a large, crisp, crunchy, densely-packed lettuce that keeps well in the fridge.

Lamb's lettuce — not a true lettuce, but tiny clumps of soft, buttery leaves that are shaped like lambs' tongues. Popular in France and Italy.

Little Gem lettuce — a small cos-type lettuce, with sweet, crisp leaves and a compact heart. Also available in red-edged varieties.

Mizuna — similar in looks to dandelion leaves, with a delicate peppery flavour.

Mustard leaf — baby leaves with an elongated shape and purple edges.

Pea shoots — with their delicate, tender fronds, they make a pretty garnish.

Radicchio — a deep-red, tightly-packed lettuce that is part of the chicory family. Mix it with other ingredients as its flavour is strong.

Red-tinged leaves — examples are escarole, lollo rosso and oakleaf. The leaves range in colour from red to deep russet-brown, with leaves becoming greener the nearer the heart you go.

Rocket — small peppery leaves with jagged edges and a fiery flavour.

Spinach — the crisp, bitter leaves add contrast when mixed with milder-tasting ones.

Watercress — this is the most widely used of all the cresses, with a tart, peppery flavour and rounded petal-like leaves.

Beyond leaves

Energy-boosting fruit and vegetables — these can offer complex carbohydrates for slow-release energy and soluble and insoluble dietary fibre, which aids sustained absorption of sugar into the blood stream.

Protein plus — turn a simple salad into a protein-boosting main meal with the addition of a little grilled steak, chicken, turkey, salmon, sea bass or other fish, or add a few stir-fried prawns. Alternatively, add tofu, a sprinkling of crumbled feta cheese, diced Brie or a few Parmesan shavings. In the West we eat more protein than our bodies need, but if you cut these ingredients into strips, shreds or dice, a little goes a long way and you can serve smaller portions without anyone really noticing. Nutritionists recommend eating just 115 g/4 oz portion of red meat per serving.

Vitamin-boosters — for boosting beta carotene, choose from orange-fleshed melons, pumpkins, carrots, papayas and mangos, dark green leafy vegetables, tomatoes and red peppers. Good sources of vitamin C include peppers, green leafy vegetables, kale, citrus fruits, berries, mangos and papayas.

Mineral-boosting nuts and seeds — these provide vitamin E, iron, zinc, magnesium, protein and fibre. Some seeds, such as flaxseeds (also called linseeds), provide omega-3 fatty acids. Nuts (except for coconut) are high in monounsaturated fats, while seeds are high in polyunsaturated fats; both are good fats. Although this increases their calories, a small sprinkle goes a long way.

Healthy whole grains — choose from wheatberries, buckwheat, bulgar wheat, wholewheat couscous, quinoa, pearl barley, oat groats and lentils. All are rich in protein, complex carbs and a wide range of vitamins and minerals. They are also high in soluble fibre to help reduce cholesterol, and insoluble fibre for healthy digestion. Quinoa is the only grain that contains all the essential amino acids. Unlike meat proteins, most grains need to be eaten with a second protein source.

How to make vinaigrette

The traditional blend for this classic French dressing is a ratio of three parts oil to one part vinegar, with a little salt and pepper plus a flavouring of your choice. These proportions can be tweaked depending on the acidity of the vinegar or strength or flavour of the oil.

The key to a good vinaigrette is to whisk the vinegar with an emulsifier such as 1 teaspoon of Dijon mustard, a very finely chopped shallot or 1 teaspoon of honey. Gradually whisk in the oil, drop by drop, until the texture is smooth and thick and the vinegar and oil have emulsified together to make a creamy dressing. The more you whisk, the thicker the dressing will be.

If the dressing is too thin or has separated, start again in a clean, small bowl with an extra teaspoon of mustard or a tablespoon of double cream or natural yogurt, then slowly whisk in the dressing until smooth once more.

Check the seasoning and the balance of the oil and vinegar once the dressing is made, and adjust if needed. Taste again once the salad is dressed. There are so few ingredients in a good vinaigrette that getting the balance right is critical.

To flavour your dressing, try whisking in a little finely chopped fresh tarragon, chives, parsley or garlic. For an Asian twist, add a dash of soy sauce and a little finely grated fresh ginger. For something with fiery heat, add deseeded and finely chopped red chilli, a few drops of Tabasco and Worcestershire sauce, or even a little Cognac. Other good flavourings include toasted and coarsely crushed coriander, cumin or fennel seeds, a little sun-dried tomato purée or a sprinkling of finely chopped aromatic herbs such as fresh mint or coriander leaves.

Choosing an oil

Olive oil is often the first choice for salad dressings. Choose from dark green extra virgin, virgin or light olive oil (a golden oil made from the last pressing). They vary hugely in flavour, depending on which country or region they come from, ranging from peppery to salty to fruity to creamy to mild. A good source of vitamin E and high in flavonoids and monounsaturated fatty acids, unheated olive oils aren't thought to raise blood cholesterol levels and may help lower them.

Nut oils, such as walnut or hazelnut oil, give a strong flavour to dressings. However, they also tend to be quite expensive. They are best mixed half-and-half with a milder oil. Sesame oil, which is made from roasted and crushed sesame seeds, has a strong, smoky flavour, and is combined mainly with Asian ingredients.

Look out for flaxseed (linseed) and hemp seed oils. Like olive oil, they are produced with minimal heat. Some are made by cold-pressing refining processes, so they retain more phytochemicals and essential fatty acids. They tend to be produced without any herbicides, pesticides, bleaches or deodorising.

Hemp oil is naturally rich in omega-3 fatty acids; a single tablespoon contains almost 100 per cent of an adult's daily recommended intake. It is also thought to contribute to your hair, skin, immune system and joint health and it is believed to have some anti-inflammatory properties.

Rice bran oil, which has a light flavour, also makes a healthy option. It is rich in vitamin E and can be used in cooking. Safflower and sunflower oils are rich in omega-6 fatty acids, but these, along with vegetable oil blends and grapeseed oil, tend to be more processed than other oils.

Keep nut and seed oils in a cool dark place, preferably in the fridge, once opened. It's best to buy them in small quantities.

Choosing a vinegar

Choose from red or white wine vinegar, or try cider, sherry or balsamic. Sherry vinegar has a rich, deep flavour, but is lighter than balsamic. True balsamic vinegar is an artisan product from Modena in Italy, and is made from pressed grape juice that has been fermented in wooden barrels for years to give it a sweet, tangy, mellow taste. It is so full of flavour that you can use it as a salad dressing on its own.

Easy vinaigrette

For a simple vinaigrette, put a tablespoon of white or red wine vinegar and 3 tablespoons of olive oil in a jam jar. Add a teaspoon each of Dijon mustard and runny honey and season with salt and pepper. Screw on the lid, then shake well. The more you shake the dressing, the more emulsified it will be. It won't be as thick as if you trickle in the oil, but it will be delicious.

All dressed up

Vinaigrette — this is the classic oil-and-vinegar salad dressing. You can flavour it with Dijon or wholegrain mustard, a finely chopped shallot or finely chopped fresh herbs, and sweeten it with a little runny honey. Whisk the ingredients together, adding the oil gradually to create a smooth emulsion.

Slimming and healthy dressings — mayonnaise and soured cream or blue cheese dressings are loaded with calories. To reduce their fat, mix them half-and-half with natural yogurt. For a more slimming dressing, mix virtually fat-free natural yogurt with chopped fresh herbs, finely chopped garlic, and crushed peppercorns or ground spices, or a mix of all three, and a small sprinkling of sweetener. For a zingy, light, vitamin C-boosting dressing, try freshly squeezed lemon, lime or orange juice seasoned with salt and pepper. A few flaxseeds (linseeds) make a healthy addition to a dressing.

Dairy-free dressings — try a mixture of orange or lemon juice, a little Dijon mustard and a splash of aged balsamic vinegar. Also try lime juice mixed with finely grated fresh ginger and soy sauce. There is a wide choice of oils, such as sunflower, olive, seed and nut oils, and vinegars, such as sherry, red or white wine.

Classic
Vinaigrette

Dairy-free
dressings

Healthy
dressings

Slimming
dressings

Refresh

Classic melon, Parma ham & pecorino salad

Per serving: 328 cals 21.3g fat 5.2g sat fat 17.2g protein 22.7g carbs 2.2g fibre

You can enjoy a lovely big bowl of this fresh-tasting salad without feeling guilty, as the melon is so deliciously low in calories! With the salty hit from the ham and pecorino and the refreshing, water-packed melon, it's a perfect lunch for a hot day.

Serves 4

* 400 g/14 oz watermelon flesh, thinly sliced
* 400 g/14 oz honeydew melon flesh, thinly sliced
* 400 g/14 oz canteloupe melon flesh, thinly sliced
* 140 g/5 oz sliced Parma ham
* 25 g/1 oz pecorino cheese shavings
* 25 g/1 oz fresh basil

Dressing

* 4 tbsp light olive oil
* 4 tbsp aged sherry vinegar
* salt and pepper

How to make it

Arrange the watermelon, honeydew melon and canteloupe melon slices on a large serving platter. Tear any large Parma ham slices in half, then fold them all over and around the melon.

To make the dressing, put the olive oil and sherry vinegar in a jam jar, season well with salt and pepper, screw on the lid and shake well. Drizzle over the melon and Parma ham.

Sprinkle on the pecorino and basil. Serve immediately.

Melon detox

Melons are low in calories, containing just 19–31 calories per 100 g/3½ oz peeled weight, depending on type. The more orange the melon's flesh, the more beneficial beta carotene it contains. Beta carotene works with vitamins C and E and minerals to help protect our cells from the harmful effects of oxidation caused by pollution, pesticide residues, smoking and stress.

Refreshing seared beef salad

Per serving: 352 cals 20g fat 3.5g sat fat 31.6g protein 15g carbs 2.9g fibre

A Thai-inspired salad with wafer-thin sliced seared steak served over
sliced peppery radishes, nutrient-boosting kale, cool mint and coriander,
all drizzled with a zesty lime dressing.

Serves 4

* ½ iceberg lettuce, leaves separated and torn into bite-sized pieces
* 200 g/7 oz radishes, thinly sliced
* 4 shallots, thinly sliced
* 85 g/3 oz kale, shredded
* 2 tbsp dried goji berries
* 25 g/1 oz fresh mint, roughly chopped
* 25 g/1 oz fresh coriander, roughly chopped
* 2 x 250 g/9 oz sirloin steaks, visible fat removed
* 4 tbsp sunflower oil
* juice of 1 lime
* 1 tbsp soy sauce
* salt and pepper

Crunch time

Put the lettuce, radishes and shallots in a serving bowl. Sprinkle over the kale, goji berries, mint and coriander, then toss gently together.

Preheat a ridged griddle pan over a high heat. Brush the steaks with 1 tablespoon of oil, then sprinkle with a little salt and pepper. Cook in the hot pan for 2 minutes on each side for medium-rare, 3 minutes for medium or 4 minutes for well done. Transfer the steaks to a plate and leave to rest for a few minutes.

Meanwhile, to make the dressing, put the lime juice, soy sauce and remaining 3 tablespoons of oil in a jam jar, screw on the lid and shake well. Drizzle over the salad, then toss together.

Divide the salad between four bowls. Thinly slice the steak and arrange it over the top, then serve immediately.

Mint for your tummy

Fresh mint leaves freshen the palate and are rich in chlorophyll, antioxidants and the essential oils menthol, menthione and menthol acetate. Mint is thought to help relieve symptoms of irritable bowel syndrome by relieving bloating and abdominal discomfort.

Light tamarind turkey salad

Per serving: 302 cals 15.2g fat 1.8g sat fat 29.2g protein 14g carbs 1.8g fibre

Tamarind gives this salad a tart, sour flavour that works wonderfully with the sweet orange juice and maple syrup. The tangy dressing doubles up as a sticky glaze for the stir-fried turkey – brilliant!

Serves 4

* 4 tbsp sunflower oil
* 450 g/1 lb raw turkey breast slices, cut into small dice
* ½ iceberg lettuce, leaves separated and torn into bite-sized pieces
* 50 g/1¾ oz chicory, leaves separated
* 85 g/3 oz kale, shredded
* 150 g/5½ oz cucumber, diced
* ½ small red onion, thinly sliced
* orange rind strips, to garnish

Dressing

* 2 tsp tamarind paste, any seeds removed
* finely grated rind and juice of 1 orange
* 2-cm/¾-inch piece of fresh ginger, peeled and finely grated
* 2 garlic cloves, finely chopped
* 4 tsp maple syrup
* salt and pepper

Mix it up

To make the dressing, put the tamarind paste, orange rind and juice, ginger, garlic and maple syrup in a small bowl, then stir in salt and pepper to taste.

To make the salad, heat 2 tablespoons of the oil in a large frying pan over a medium—high heat. Add the turkey and stir-fry for 5 minutes, or until golden and cooked through; cut into the middle of a piece to check that the meat is no longer pink and that the juices are clear and piping hot. Add half the dressing and fry for 2—3 minutes more, or until the turkey is glazed and shiny. Transfer the turkey to a plate and set aside.

Put the lettuce, chicory and kale in a salad bowl and sprinkle over the cucumber and onion.

Mix the remaining 2 tablespoons of oil into the remaining dressing. Drizzle over the salad, then toss gently together and scatter the warm, glazed turkey on top. Garnish with the orange rind and serve.

Good for your heart!

Eating lots of fruit and vegetables can help protect you from heart disease and reduce your risk of stroke by up to 30 per cent.

Fruity Florida chicken salad

Per serving: 229 cals   8.4g fat   1g sat fat   21.6g protein   18.6g carbs   4g fibre

This super-healthy take on coleslaw is bursting with zingy citrus fruit, crunchy white cabbage and thin shreds of kale, all tossed in a light lime vinaigrette instead of a classic coleslaw mayonnaise dressing.

Serves 4

* 2 tbsp sunflower oil
* 250 g/9 oz sliced mini skinless chicken breast fillets
* ¼ tsp dried crushed red chillies
* 1 pink grapefruit, peeled with a knife and cut into segments, membrane reserved
* 1 orange, peeled with a knife and cut into segments, membrane reserved
* 1 small mango, halved, pitted, peeled and diced
* 225 g/8 oz white cabbage, cored and thinly shredded
* 55 g/2 oz kale, thinly shredded
* salt and pepper

Dressing

* juice of 1 lime
* 1 tsp Dijon mustard
* 2-cm/¾-inch piece of fresh ginger, peeled and finely grated

Make it now!

Heat 1 tablespoon of the oil in a frying pan over a medium—high heat. Add the chicken, sprinkle with the chillies and season with a little salt and pepper. Fry for 8—10 minutes, turning once or twice, or until golden and cooked through; cut into the middle of a piece to check that the meat is no longer pink and that the juices are clear and piping hot. Transfer the chicken to a plate.

Put the grapefruit and orange segments in a salad bowl, then add the mango, cabbage and kale and toss together.

To make the dressing, squeeze the juice from the citrus membranes into a jam jar. Add the lime juice, mustard, ginger and remaining 1 tablespoon of oil, then season to taste with salt and pepper. Screw on the lid and shake well. Drizzle over the salad, then toss gently together.

Divide the salad between four bowls, cut the fried chicken into shreds, scatter over the top, then serve.

Light tamarind
turkey salad

page 18

Fruity Florida
chicken salad

page 19

Grilled sea bass & citrus salad

Bursting with vitamins and minerals, this light, zesty salad with lime-marinated grilled sea bass will leave you feeling fresh and ready to go!

Serves 4

* 85 g/3 oz baby spinach
* 40 g/1½ oz lamb's lettuce
* 40 g/1½ oz ruby chard leaves
* 2 ruby grapefruits, peeled with a knife and cut into segments, membrane reserved
* 1 orange, peeled with a knife and cut into segments, membrane reserved
* 4 sea bass fillets
* finely grated rind and juice of 1 lime
* 3 tbsp olive oil
* 1 tsp runny honey
* salt and pepper
* 2 tbsp finely chopped fresh coriander, to garnish

Time to get started

Put the spinach, lamb's lettuce and chard leaves in a salad bowl. Scatter on the grapefruit and orange segments. Squeeze the juice from the citrus membranes into a jam jar and reserve.

Preheat the grill to hot and line the grill pan with foil. Arrange the sea bass flesh side up on the foil, sprinkle with the lime rind and juice and season with salt and pepper. Turn the fish over, season with salt and pepper and drizzle with 1 tablespoon of olive oil. Grill for 6—8 minutes, turning once, or until the skin is browned and the fish is opaque and flakes when pressed.

To make the dressing, add the remaining olive oil and the honey to the fruit juice in the jar, season to taste with salt and pepper, screw on the lid and shake well. Drizzle over the salad and toss gently together, then divide between four plates.

Break each fish fillet into bite-sized pieces, then arrange them on top of the salads. Sprinkle with the coriander, spoon over any juices from the grill pan, then serve immediately.

Per serving: 260 cals   6.7g fat   1.2g sat fat   30g protein   20.7g carbs   3.5g fibre

Go citrus crazy!

The colourful citrus family includes oranges, kumquats, lemons, limes, grapefruits, tangerines, pomelos and other hybrid citrus fruits, and contains some of the richest fruit sources of vitamin C. One medium-to-large orange provides twice the Recommended National Intake (RNI) of this vitamin. Vital to aid the absorption of iron, which is especially important if you eat little meat, vitamin C also helps us fight infection and boosts the immune system. It is thought it may help with nasal inflammation, so reducing the symptoms of a cold, catarrh, hayfever and even rheumatism. A high intake of vitamin C may also lower the risk of coronary heart disease by up to 40 per cent and slow down the effects of skin ageing.Pink grapefruit and blood oranges also contain good amounts of beta carotene, while lemons contain limonene, a phytochemical that is thought to help protect against cancer.

Seafood super salad

Per serving: 272 cals   15.7g fat   2.3g sat fat   22g protein   10.2g carbs   0.5g fibre

Seafood is as refreshing as sea air – but you don't have to travel to the coast
to enjoy this deliciously fresh-tasting salad!

Serves 4

* 250 g/9 oz live mussels, scrubbed and debearded
* 350 g/12 oz live scallops, shucked and cleaned
* 250 g/9 oz cleaned and prepared squid, cut into rings and tentacles
* 1 red onion, thinly sliced
* 1 lemon, cut into 4 wedges, to serve

Dressing

* 4 tbsp extra virgin olive oil
* 2 tbsp white wine vinegar
* 1 tbsp lemon juice
* 1 garlic clove, finely chopped
* 1 tbsp finely chopped fresh flat-leaf parsley, plus 1 tbsp to garnish
* salt and pepper

Toss your salad

Discard any mussels with broken shells or that refuse to close when tapped. Put the remaining mussels in a colander and rinse well under cold running water. Tip them into a large saucepan, add a little water and cook, covered, over a high heat, shaking occasionally, for 3—4 minutes, or until they have opened. Discard any that remain closed. Strain the mussels, reserving the cooking liquid, then refresh them under cold running water, drain and set aside.

Return the reserved cooking liquid to the pan and bring to the boil. Add the scallops and squid and cook for 3 minutes. Remove from the heat and drain. Refresh them under cold running water, drain again and set aside.

Remove the cooked mussels from their shells and put them in a bowl. Add the scallops and squid, then leave to cool. Cover with cling film and chill in the refrigerator for 45 minutes. Divide the seafood between four bowls, add the onion and toss gently together.

To make the dressing, put the oil, wine vinegar, lemon juice, garlic and parsley in a jam jar, season with salt and pepper, screw on the lid and shake well. Drizzle over the salads and garnish with the parsley. Serve immediately, with the lemon wedges for squeezing over.

Super seafood

Seafood is generally rich in protein, vitamins and minerals, yet low in calories. Shellfish is a good source of the trace minerals selenium and zinc, which work with vitamin E for normal body growth and fertility.

Chilli calamari salad

Per serving: 506 cals 37.7g fat 5.5g sat fat 29.2g protein 13g carbs 1.2g fibre

A tangy lime-dressed mixture of seared squid, red chilli and spring onions, served with cool, crisp iron-rich leaves, guaranteed to wake up and refresh those taste-buds.

Serves 4

* 700 g/1 lb 9 oz cleaned and prepared squid, cut into tubes and tentacles
* 3 tbsp olive oil
* 1 red chilli, deseeded and thinly sliced
* 2 spring onions, finely chopped
* a squeeze of lemon juice, plus lemon wedges, to serve
* 100 g/3½ oz watercress
* 70 g/2½ oz baby spinach
* salt and pepper

Dressing

* 100 ml/3½ fl oz olive oil
* juice of 1 lime
* 1 tsp runny honey
* 2 shallots, thinly sliced
* 1 tomato, peeled, deseeded and finely chopped
* 1 garlic clove, crushed

Make it now!

To make the dressing, put all the ingredients in a small bowl, season to taste with salt and pepper, mix together well, cover and refrigerate until required.

Cut the squid tubes into 5-cm/2-inch pieces, then score diamond patterns lightly across the flesh using the tip of a sharp knife. Heat the oil in a large frying pan over a high heat. Add the squid pieces and tentacles and stir-fry for 1 minute. Add the chilli and spring onions and stir-fry for a further minute. Season well with salt and pepper and add a good squeeze of lemon juice.

Put the watercress and spinach in a salad bowl, then add the cooked squid. Drizzle over enough dressing to coat lightly and toss gently together. Serve immediately, with the lemon wedges for squeezing over.

Squid's in!

Squid can provide the body with 90 per cent of the copper it needs. Copper is a trace mineral that plays a role in the absorption, storage and metabolism of iron and the formation of red blood cells (RBC). Copper deficiency may show in the form of anaemia.

Cool watermelon, goat's cheese & rocket salad

Per serving: 207 cals   11g fat   7.1g sat fat   11g protein   19.4g carbs   1.8g fibre

The delicate creaminess of the goat's cheese in this salad complements the citrus- and chilli-dressed watermelon to make a deliciously quick and rehydrating summer salad that will have you coming back for more.

Serves 4

* 800 g/1 lb 12 oz watermelon flesh, cut into large cubes
* grated rind and juice of 2 large limes, plus lime wedges, to serve
* ½–1 red chilli, deseeded and finely chopped
* 55 g/2 oz fresh coriander, roughly chopped
* 70 g/2½ oz rocket
* 115 g/4 oz firm goat's cheese, cut into cubes
* salt and pepper

Mix it up

Put the watermelon in a large salad bowl. Sprinkle with the lime rind and juice and the chilli, then season with a little salt and pepper and toss gently together.

Sprinkle over the coriander, rocket and goat's cheese and gently toss together. Serve with lime wedges.

Thirst-quenching watermelon

It is recommended that we drink six to eight glasses of water a day, but don't forget that our foods can contribute to our water intake too. Watermelon is around 80 per cent water, plus ripe watermelons contain a powerful antioxidant, glutathione, which is known to help boost the immune system and fight infection.

Roasted pepper pep-up salad

Per serving: 321 cals 27.5g fat 5.7g sat fat 7.6g protein 12.3g carbs 2.8g fibre

Capture the taste of the Mediterranean with this roasted antioxidant-rich pepper salad.

Serves 4

* 2 red peppers, halved and deseeded
* 2 yellow peppers, halved and deseeded
* 1 red onion, roughly chopped
* 2 garlic cloves, finely chopped
* 6 tbsp olive oil
* 100 g/3½ oz mini mozzarella cheese pearls, drained
* 2 tbsp roughly torn fresh basil
* 2 tbsp balsamic vinegar
* salt and pepper

Time to get started

Preheat the oven to 190°C/375°F/Gas Mark 5. Put the peppers cut side up in a shallow roasting tin. Scatter over the onion and garlic, season well with salt and pepper and drizzle over 3 tablespoons of the olive oil. Roast for 40 minutes, or until the peppers are tender. Leave to cool.

Arrange the cold peppers in a serving dish and pour over any juices left in the roasting tin. Scatter over the mozzarella and basil.

To make the dressing, whisk together the remaining olive oil and the balsamic vinegar, then drizzle over the peppers. Cover and leave to marinate in the refrigerator for at least 2 hours before serving.

Power peppers

All peppers are rich in vitamins A, C and K, but red peppers are simply bursting with them. Antioxidant vitamins A and C help to prevent cell damage, cancer and diseases related to ageing, and they support immune function. They also reduce inflammation such as that found in arthritis and asthma.

Oh-so-good-for-you Greek feta salad

Per serving: 208 cals   17.4g fat   5.8g sat fat   5.8g protein   8.8g carbs   1.8g fibre

A Mediterranean diet, rich in olive oil, sun-kissed vegetables and lemons, has long been recognised as healthy, and this simple, tasty salad is no exception. But it will only taste as good as the tomatoes you choose.

Serves 4

* 25 g/1 oz blanched vine leaves, drained
* 300 g/10½ oz tomatoes, thinly sliced
* 150 g/5½ oz cucumber, peeled and thinly sliced
* 1 small red onion, thinly sliced
* 115 g/4 oz feta cheese (drained weight), cut into cubes
* 32 black olives, stoned

Dressing

* 3 tbsp extra virgin olive oil
* 1 tbsp lemon juice
* ½ tsp dried oregano
* salt and pepper

How to make it

Arrange the vine leaves on four plates. Scatter over the tomatoes, cucumber and onion, then the feta and olives.

To make the dressing, put the oil, lemon juice and dried oregano in a jam jar, screw on the lid and shake well. Drizzle over the salad, season to taste with salt and pepper, then serve immediately.

Feta is fab

Feta cheese is made with sheep's or goat's milk. It contains calcium, which helps keep your bones strong and can help to prevent osteoporosis. It also contains vitamin B12, which helps with brain function. So say yes to feta!

Spiced beetroot & cucumber tzatziki

Per serving: 50 cals   0.8g fat   0.5g sat fat   4.8g protein   6.6g carbs   1.5g fibre

These mini bites make a perfect starter, and are delicious served as part of a mixed selection of nibbles to go with drinks.

Serves 4

* 115 g/4 oz cooked beetroot in natural juices (drained weight), drained and diced
* 150 g/5½ oz cucumber, diced
* 40 g/1½ oz radishes, diced
* 1 spring onion, finely chopped
* 12 Little Gem lettuce leaves

Dressing

* 150 g/5½ oz 2 per cent fat Greek-style natural yogurt
* ¼ tsp ground cumin
* ½ tsp runny honey
* 2 tbsp finely chopped fresh mint
* salt and pepper

Toss your salad

To make the dressing, put the yogurt, cumin and honey in a bowl, then stir in the mint and season to taste with salt and pepper.

Add the beetroot, cucumber, radishes and spring onion, then toss gently together.

Arrange the lettuce leaves on a plate. Spoon a little of the salad into each leaf. Serve immediately.

Love lettuce

The outer leaves of a lettuce contain the most beta carotene and vitamin C, with small amounts of folate and iron. Lettuce is thought by herbalists to calm the nerves and aid sleep.

Bitter greens with palate-cleansing citrus dressing

Per serving: 103 cals   7g fat   1.2g sat fat   1.5g protein   9.6g carbs   1.8g fibre

Capture the essence of summer with this baby leaf salad tossed with bitter frisée lettuce in a zesty orange and lemon dressing with a hint of soy.

Serves 4

* ¼ frisée lettuce, torn into bite-sized pieces
* 55 g/2 oz baby spinach
* 70 g/2½ oz mixed baby leaf salad
* 115 g/4 oz blueberries
* a few edible nasturtium and viola flowers (optional), to garnish

Dressing

* finely grated rind and juice of ½ small orange, plus extra finely grated rind, to garnish
* finely grated rind and juice of ½ unwaxed lemon, plus extra finely grated rind, to garnish
* 1 tbsp light soy sauce
* 2 tbsp rice bran oil
* 1 tsp runny honey
* pepper

Flower power

Put the frisée lettuce, spinach and baby salad leaves in a large salad bowl. Sprinkle over the blueberries.

To make the dressing, put the orange and lemon rind and juice, soy sauce, oil and honey in a jam jar, season to taste with pepper, screw on the lid and shake well. Drizzle over the salad, then gently toss together. Serve on four plates, garnished with the flowers, if using, and orange and lemon rind.

Brilliant blueberries

With their high antioxidant levels, blueberries not only help to protect us against cancer, but also to stabilise brain function and protect neural tissue from oxidative stress (which may improve memory and learning and reduce symptoms of depression).

Big borlotti bean, tomato & onion salad with eggs

Per serving: 503 cals   26.6g fat   2g sat fat   23g protein   44.5g carbs   17g fibre

The lemon dressing gives this salad a refreshing, zesty flavour and complements the earthy beans perfectly.

Serves 4

* 250 g/9 oz dried borlotti beans, soaked overnight or for at least 8 hours
* 2 large garlic cloves, crushed
* juice of 2 lemons
* 6 tbsp extra virgin olive oil
* 1 small onion, finely chopped
* 2 tomatoes, deseeded and finely chopped
* 40 g/1½ oz fresh flat-leaf parsley, finely chopped
* 1 tsp cumin seeds, crushed
* salt and pepper

Garnish

* 4 eggs
* 1 lemon, cut into 4 wedges
* pinch of sumac or dried crushed red chillies

Time to get started

Drain and rinse the beans, put them in a large saucepan, cover with fresh cold water and bring to the boil. Boil rapidly for at least 10 minutes, then remove from the heat, drain and rinse again. Add fresh cold water, bring to the boil, then simmer for 1½–2 hours, or until tender, topping up with boiling water if needed. Drain and tip into a shallow serving dish.

For the garnish, put the eggs in a saucepan and pour in enough cold water to cover them by 1 cm/½ inch. Bring to the boil, then reduce to a simmer and cook for 8 minutes. Drain immediately, cool quickly under cold running water, then peel and cut into quarters.

Lightly crush some of the warm beans with the back of a spoon. Add the garlic, lemon juice, olive oil and 1 teaspoon of salt while the beans are warm, and mix together. Add the onion, tomatoes, parsley and cumin and season to taste with pepper, then toss gently together. Arrange the hard-boiled eggs and lemon wedges on top, sprinkle with the sumac and serve.

Gingered carrot & pomegranate salad

Per serving: 179 cals 10.7g fat 1.5g sat fat 2g protein 20g carbs 4.2g fibre

Turn a humble carrot into an exotic, fresh-tasting salad with a little Middle Eastern magic with the help of jewel-like pomegranate!

Serves 4

* 350 g/12 oz carrots, finely grated
* 5-cm/2-inch piece of fresh ginger, peeled and finely grated
* 1 small pomegranate, quartered
* 50 g/1¾ oz ready-to-eat sprouting seeds, such as alfalfa and radish sprouts

Dressing

* 3 tbsp light olive oil
* 3 tsp red wine vinegar
* 3 tsp pomegranate molasses
* salt and pepper

Mix it up

Put the carrots and ginger in a salad bowl. Flex the pomegranate pieces to pop out the seeds, prising any stubborn ones out with the tip of a small knife, and add to the bowl.

To make the dressing, put the oil, vinegar and pomegranate molasses in a jam jar, season with salt and pepper, screw on the lid and shake well. Drizzle over the salad and toss gently together. Cover and leave to marinate in the refrigerator for 30 minutes.

Sprinkle the sprouting seeds over the salad and serve.

Pomegranate jewels

The pomegranate's glistening ruby-like seeds might be tiny, but they pack a punch. They are rich in flavonoids and polyphenols, antioxidants thought to help protect against heart disease and cancer.

Zesty avocado, pineapple & pink grapefruit salad

Per serving: 150 cals   6g fat   0.8g sat fat   2g protein   26g carbs   5.5g fibre

Wake up those taste-buds with this super zingy fresh fruity salad. Prettily served in an iceberg lettuce cup, it makes a perfect starter or side dish.

Serves 4

* 2 pink grapefruits, peeled with a knife and cut into segments, membrane reserved
* ½ pineapple, sliced, peeled, cored and diced
* 1 large avocado, halved, pitted, peeled and diced
* finely grated rind and juice of 1 lime
* 2 tbsp finely chopped fresh mint
* 4 outer iceberg lettuce leaves

How to make it

Halve each grapefruit segment, then put them in a salad bowl. Squeeze the juice from the membrane over the segments. Add the pineapple and avocado, sprinkle over the lime rind and juice and mint, then gently toss together.

Arrange a lettuce leaf on each of four small plates. Spoon salad into the centre of each lettuce leaf and serve immediately.

Pineapple pick-me-up

Vitamin C-rich pineapple and grapefruit help boost the body's immune system and the production of collagen needed for healthy skin, bones, cartilage, teeth and gums. Vitamin C may even also be a key protective element against cardiovascular disease, cancer and asthma.

Baby leaf remedy salad with raspberry dressing

Per serving: 150 cals 11.2g fat 1.4g sat fat 2.4g protein 12g carbs 4.2g fibre

A fresh raspberry dressing is gently tossed with tummy-soothing summer salad leaves and antioxidant-rich goji berries.

Serves 4

* 125 g/4½ oz bistro salad (a mix of red-stemmed baby red chard, bull's blood chard and lamb's lettuce)
* 25 g/1 oz rocket
* 25 g/1 oz pea shoots
* 175 g/6 oz raspberries
* 3 tbsp dried goji berries

Dressing

* 1 tsp runny honey
* 1 tbsp red wine vinegar
* 3 tbsp light olive oil
* salt and pepper

Pretty in pink

Put the bistro salad, rocket and pea shoots in a salad bowl, then toss gently together.

To make the dressing, put 55 g/2 oz raspberries, the honey, vinegar and oil in a blender, season to taste with salt and pepper, then whizz until smooth.

Serve the salad leaves on small plates, sprinkled with the remaining raspberries and the goji berries, with the dressing for drizzling over.

Raspberry boost

Raspberries are rich in vitamin C. Herbalists also suggest using raspberry vinegar to help coughs.

Exotic coconut cooler

Per serving: 390 cals   25.9g fat   22.3g sat fat   5.2g protein   41g carbs   10.7g fibre

Awaken those taste-buds and transport them to Jamaica with this tropical salad, which combines juicy, lightly perfumed mango, sweet, refreshing pineapple and crunchy, fresh coconut speckled with tiny ruby goji berries.

Serves 4

* 1 small coconut
* finely grated rind and juice of 1 lime
* 1 small pineapple, sliced, peeled, cored and diced
* 1 large mango, halved, pitted, peeled and diced
* 150 g/5½ oz cucumber, peeled, halved lengthways, deseeded and thickly sliced
* 3 tbsp dried goji berries
* 50 g/1¾ oz fresh coriander, finely chopped

Tropical dreams

Pierce one of the three eyes in the base of the coconut using a skewer, then drain out the liquid, strain it through a sieve and reserve. Break the rest of the coconut into pieces.

To make the dressing, mix the coconut milk and lime rind and juice together in a salad bowl. Prise the flesh away from the hard coconut shell using a small pointed knife, then pare it into thin shavings using a swivel-bladed vegetable peeler, to make 85 g/3 oz.

Add the coconut shavings to the dressing, then add the pineapple, mango, cucumber, goji berries and coriander and toss gently together. Spoon into four bowls and serve immediately.

The five-a-day way!

At least 50 per cent of your calories should come from plant-based foods, so aim to eat a minimum of five portions of fruit and veg every day.

Energy

Sweet & sour crispy pork with gingered noodle salad

Per serving: 461 cals 10.5g fat 1.7g sat fat 40g protein 48g carbs 4.4g fibre

Made up of a good mix of complex carbs and fibre, this light, fresh-tasting salad will provide a slow-release energy boost. It can be prepared the night before, stored in the fridge, then taken to work in a plastic container for a healthy office lunch.

Serves 4

* 600 g/1 lb 5 oz lean pork leg escalopes
* 200 g/7 oz dried wholewheat Chinese noodles
* 200 g/7 oz Chinese leaves, shredded
* 115 g/4 oz carrots, cut into thin matchsticks
* 115 g/4 oz mangetout, thinly sliced
* 2 spring onions, finely chopped
* 2-cm/¾-inch piece of fresh ginger, peeled and finely grated

Dressing

* finely grated rind and juice of ½ orange
* 2 tbsp sunflower oil
* 2 tbsp soy sauce
* 1 tbsp runny honey
* 1 tbsp rice vinegar
* 1 tsp star anise pieces, ground
* 2 garlic cloves, finely chopped

Oodles of noodles

Preheat the grill to high and line the grill pan with foil. To make the dressing, put the orange rind and juice, oil, soy sauce, honey, vinegar, star anise and garlic in a jam jar, screw on the lid and shake well.

Arrange the pork on the grill pan in a single layer and spoon over 3 tablespoons of the dressing. Grill for 12—15 minutes, turning the pork and spooning over the juices once or twice, until browned and cooked through.

Meanwhile, cook the noodles according to the packet instructions. Drain into a sieve, rinse with cold water, then drain again. Put them in a salad bowl, pour over the remaining dressing and leave to cool.

Add the Chinese leaves, carrots, mangetout, spring onions and ginger to the salad bowl and toss gently together. Thinly slice the pork and arrange it over the salad, then serve.

Foods for energy

We need energy to breathe, move, exercise, grow and pump blood around our bodies. It comes mainly from carbohydrates, but also from fat and protein. Carbs should provide at least 50 per cent, fat no more than 35 per cent and protein a maximum of 15 per cent of our daily diet.

Spinach & pancetta power salad

Per serving: 413 cals 36.5g fat 8.9g sat fat 16.2g protein 6.4g carbs 3.7g fibre

The sweet, sticky dressing perfectly enhances the smoky pancetta and slightly bitter spinach leaves in this filling salad.

Serves 4

* 2 tbsp olive oil
* 275 g/9¾ oz baby spinach
* 150 g/5½ oz pancetta, diced
* 280 g/10 oz mixed wild mushrooms, sliced

Dressing

* 1 tbsp balsamic vinegar
* 1 tsp Dijon mustard
* 1 tsp maple syrup
* 5 tbsp olive oil
* salt and pepper

Toss your salad

To make the dressing, put the vinegar, mustard, maple syrup and olive oil in a jam jar, season to taste with salt and pepper, screw on the lid and shake well.

Put the spinach in a salad bowl. Heat the olive oil in a large frying pan over a medium—high heat. Add the pancetta and fry for 3 minutes, stirring. Add the mushrooms and fry for 3—4 minutes, or until the pancetta is cooked and the mushrooms are tender.

Pour the dressing into the frying pan, then immediately tip the fried mixture and dressing into the salad bowl. Toss well and serve.

Power pancetta

Pancetta is traditional Italian bacon. It is high in fat, so it is not advisable to eat large amounts of it. However, in limited quantities it will provide a good deal of energy.

Seared beef salad with horseradish ricotta dressing

Per serving: 362 cals 12g fat 5g sat fat 35g protein 34g carbs 6.4g fibre

A man-sized salad packed with complex carbs for slow-release energy, protein for muscle growth and repair, and iron for healthy blood cells to power you through any exercise regime or hectic work schedule.

Serves 4

* 500 g/1 lb 2 oz baby new potatoes, thickly sliced
* 225 g/8 oz cherry tomatoes, halved
* 115 g/4 oz baby spinach
* 1 red onion, finely chopped
* 225 g/8 oz cooked beetroot in natural juices (drained weight), drained and diced
* 2 tbsp balsamic vinegar
* 2 x 250 g/9 oz sirloin steaks, visible fat removed
* 2 tsp olive oil
* 1 tsp multi-coloured peppercorns, roughly crushed

Dressing

* 115 g/4 oz ricotta cheese
* 4 tbsp low-fat natural yogurt
* 1—2 tsp horseradish sauce
* salt and pepper

Beef up your salad

Put the potatoes in the top of a steamer, cover and set over a saucepan of simmering water. Steam for 6—8 minutes, or until tender. Leave to cool.

Put the cherry tomatoes, spinach, onion and beetroot in a salad bowl. Drizzle over the vinegar and toss gently together.

Preheat a ridged griddle pan over a high heat. Brush the steaks with the oil, then sprinkle with the crushed peppercorns. Cook in the hot pan for 2 minutes on each side for medium-rare, 3 minutes for medium and 4 minutes for well done. Transfer the steaks to a plate and leave to rest for a few minutes.

To make the dressing, put the ricotta and yogurt in a salad bowl, stir in the horseradish, then season to taste with salt and pepper. Add the potatoes and toss gently together. Divide the spinach salad between four plates, then spoon the potato salad in the centre. Thinly slice the steak and arrange it over the top, then serve.

Yes you can enjoy steak!

Beef steak contains a wide range of minerals, but is particularly rich in iron needed for haemoglobin, the pigment in our red blood cells that carries oxygen around the body and works with zinc for maintaining and replicating each person's individual DNA and RNA. Zinc is also essential for normal growth of the body and boosting the immune system.

Sustaining Caesar salad with maple chicken

Per serving: 464 cals 20g fat 5.2g sat fat 52g protein 20g carbs 3.9g fibre

What to eat before you do sport can be a dilemma. You need something that is light but will give you enough energy to see you through your exercise. This chicken salad offers a good mix of protein, monounsaturated fats, vegetables and carbs. Aim to eat at least one hour before exercising, then after exercise start replenishing glycogen stores with a high-carbohydrate, low-fat snack within 30 minutes.

Serves 4

* 115 g/4 oz wholemeal bread, diced
* little low-fat cooking spray
* 2 tsp Dijon mustard
* 2 garlic cloves, finely chopped
* 1 tbsp maple syrup
* 3 tbsp olive oil
* juice of 1 lemon
* 500 g/1 lb 2 oz skinless chicken breast fillets, thinly sliced
* 55 g/2 oz Parmesan cheese
* 4 Romaine lettuce hearts, leaves separated and torn into bite-sized pieces

Dressing

* 2 eggs
* 1 tsp Worcestershire sauce
* salt and pepper

Make it chicken tonight

Preheat the oven to 200°C/400°F/Gas Mark 6. Put the bread on a baking tray in a single layer, spray with low-fat cooking spray, then bake for 8–10 minutes, turning once, until golden brown and crisp.

Put half the mustard, half the chopped garlic, all the maple syrup, 1 tablespoon of olive oil and the juice of half a lemon in a shallow dish and mix together. Add the chicken and toss to coat. Cover and set aside for no more than 5 minutes.

Meanwhile, to make the dressing, put the eggs in a small saucepan, just cover with cold water, then bring to the boil and simmer for 1 minute. Drain and cool under cold running water. Crack a little of the shell off each egg, then use a teaspoon to scoop the soft egg into a blender. Add the remaining mustard, garlic and lemon juice and the Worcestershire sauce. Crumble 25 g/1 oz of the Parmesan and add it to the blender with a little salt and pepper. Whizz until smooth, then drizzle in the remaining 2 tablespoons of olive oil with the motor running, and whizz again.

Preheat a ridged griddle pan over a high heat. Cook the glazed chicken in the hot pan, in batches if necessary, for 8–10 minutes, or until cooked through, turning halfway through. Cut into the middle of a slice to check that the meat is no longer pink and the juices run clear.

Meanwhile, toss the lettuce with half the dressing, then spoon it into four bowls. Thinly shave the remaining Parmesan. Top the salad with the hot chicken and croûtons, drizzle with the remaining dressing and sprinkle with the Parmesan shavings.

Seared beef
salad with
horseradish
ricotta dressing

page 54

Sustaining
Caesar salad
with maple
chicken

page 55

Warming new potato & salmon salad

Rather than fattening butter or mayo, this warm potato salad is tossed with a tangy lemon and olive oil dressing, then topped with kale, pea shoots and salmon for a sustaining main meal.

Serves 4

* 650 g/1 lb 7 oz baby new potatoes, halved or thickly sliced if large
* 450 g/1 lb salmon fillet
* 1 red onion, thinly sliced
* ½ iceberg lettuce, torn into bite-sized pieces
* 115 g/4 oz kale, shredded
* 85 g/3 oz pea shoots
* salt and pepper

Dressing

* 4 tbsp olive oil
* juice of 1 lemon
* 2 tsp runny honey
* 1 tbsp capers, drained and chopped

How to make it

Put cold water in the base of a steamer, bring to the boil, then add the potatoes and bring back to the boil. Put the salmon in the top of the steamer in a single layer, season with salt and pepper, then put it on the steamer base, cover and steam for 10 minutes, or until the salmon is cooked. Remove the steamer top and cook the potatoes for 4—5 minutes more, or until tender.

Meanwhile, to make the dressing, put the oil, lemon juice and honey in a salad bowl, mix together well, then stir in the capers and season with salt and pepper.

Add the onion to the dressing, then add the hot potatoes and toss gently together.

Divide the lettuce and kale between four bowls and spoon over the potato mixture. Flake the salmon into large pieces, discarding any skin and bones, sprinkle over the salad, then top with the pea shoots and serve immediately.

Per serving: 519 cals 29.2g fat 5.3g sat fat 28.3g protein 35.3g carbs 6.2g fibre

Artichoke & prosciutto salad

Per serving: 345 cals 22.4g fat 3.7g sat fat 10.1g protein 27.5g carbs 9g fibre

This is a deliciously fresh, summery salad with a garlicky mustard dressing. There's no fiddly artichoke preparation; simply open a can and enjoy their delicate taste with protein-rich, wafer-thin slices of prosciutto.

Serves 4

* 275 g/9¾ oz canned artichoke hearts in oil, drained and cut into quarters
* 500 g/1 lb 2 oz small tomatoes, cut into wedges
* 25 g/1 oz sun-dried tomatoes in oil, drained and cut into very thin strips
* 40 g/1½ oz sliced prosciutto, cut into strips
* 25 g/1 oz black olives, stoned and halved
* 40 g/1½ oz fresh basil, torn, plus extra to garnish
* 150 g/5½ oz crusty white bread, to serve

Dressing

* 3 tbsp olive oil
* 1 tbsp white wine vinegar
* 1 garlic clove, crushed
* ½ tsp mild mustard
* 1 tsp runny honey
* salt and pepper

Toss your salad

Put the artichokes, tomatoes, sun-dried tomatoes, prosciutto, olives and basil in a salad bowl.

To make the dressing, put the oil, vinegar, garlic, mustard and honey in a jam jar, season to taste with salt and pepper, screw on the lid and shake well. Drizzle over the salad and toss gently together.

Garnish with the reserved basil and serve immediately with crusty bread.

Tuna, lentil & potato energizer salad

Per serving: 554 cals   25.7g fat   3.6g sat fat   37g protein   44g carbs   10.2g fibre

A fresh salad power-packed with lentils, potatoes and tuna to give you all the energy you need for an afternoon of work or play.

Serves 4

* 200 g/7 oz puy or brown lentils
* 2 tbsp olive oil, plus extra for brushing
* 300 g/10½ oz baby new potatoes, halved
* 1 Little Gem lettuce
* 4 x 100 g/3½ oz tuna steaks
* 300 g/10½ oz cherry tomatoes, halved
* 40 g/1½ oz rocket

Dressing

* 5 tbsp fruity olive oil
* 1 tbsp balsamic vinegar
* 2 tsp red wine vinegar
* 1 tsp smooth Dijon mustard
* 1 tsp runny honey

Seaside sensation

Boil the lentils in a saucepan of water for 25 minutes, or until tender. Drain, tip into a salad bowl and stir in the olive oil.

Put the potatoes in a saucepan and cover with cold water. Bring to the boil, cover and simmer for 15 minutes, or until tender. Drain well.

Meanwhile, break the outer lettuce leaves off the Little Gem and cut the heart into eight pieces. Arrange on four plates.

To make the dressing, put all the ingredients in a jam jar, screw on the lid and shake well.

Preheat a ridged griddle pan over a high heat. Brush the tuna with olive oil. Cook it in the hot pan for 3 minutes for rare or 5 minutes for medium, turning once. Transfer it to a plate and cut each steak into six chunks.

Arrange the lentils, tuna, potatoes and tomatoes over the lettuce, sprinkle over the rocket and spoon over the dressing. Serve immediately.

Terrific tuna

Tuna is a good source of omega-3 fatty acids, essential fatty acids that are thought to help reduce the risk of heart disease and arthritis and aid with brain and cognitive function.

Warm red lentil salad

Per serving: 336 cals 21g fat 8.6g sat fat 16.4g protein 19.3g carbs 4.3g fibre

Herby dressed lentils make a hearty base to a salad. Their starches are digested and absorbed slowly by the body, giving a sustained energy boost, while their soluble fibre is thought to help reduce blood cholesterol levels.

Serves 4

* 2 tbsp olive oil
* 2 tsp cumin seeds
* 2 garlic cloves, crushed
* 2-cm/¾-inch piece of fresh ginger, peeled and finely grated
* 300 g/10½ oz split red lentils
* 700 ml/1¼ pints vegetable stock
* 2 tbsp roughly chopped fresh mint
* 2 tbsp roughly chopped fresh coriander
* 2 red onions, thinly sliced
* 200 g/7 oz baby spinach
* 1 tsp hazelnut oil
* 150 g/5½ oz soft goat's cheese
* 4 tbsp Greek-style yogurt
* pepper

Toss your salad

Heat 1 tablespoon of olive oil in a large saucepan over a medium heat. Add the cumin, garlic and ginger and stir-fry for 2 minutes. Stir in the lentils, then add the stock a ladleful at a time, simmering and stirring occasionally until each ladleful has been absorbed before adding the next one — this will take about 20 minutes in all. Remove from the heat and stir in the herbs.

Meanwhile, heat the remaining 1 tablespoon of olive oil in a frying pan over a medium—low heat. Add the onions and cook, stirring often, for 10 minutes, or until soft and lightly browned.

Put the spinach and hazelnut oil in a bowl and toss gently together. Divide between four shallow bowls.

Put the goat's cheese and yogurt in a small bowl, season to taste with pepper, and mash.

Spoon the lentils on to the spinach, top with the onions, then spoon on the goat's cheese and yogurt and serve.

Love your lentils

Lentils are nutritious and economical. They're low in fat and free from cholesterol, but they are a rich source of protein, dietary fibre, B vitamins and essential amino acids and a useful source of folic acid. It is thought they can help to lower cholesterol.

Roasted tomato wholewheat pasta salad

Per serving: 473 cals 28.7g fat 5g sat fat 13.8g protein 43g carbs 8.3g fibre

Wholewheat pasta has long been a favourite energy-boosting base for people doing a lot of sport, as exercising muscles rely on carbohydrate as their main source of fuel.

Serves 4

* 600 g/1 lb 5 oz tomatoes in various colours and sizes, halved
* 2 garlic cloves, finely chopped
* 6 tbsp olive oil
* 225 g/8 oz dried wholewheat pasta, such as mafalda corta or quills
* 85 g/3 oz baby spinach
* salt and pepper

Spinach pesto

* 50 g/1¾ oz fresh basil, plus extra leaves to garnish
* 25 g/1 oz pine nuts
* 25 g/1 oz Parmesan cheese, finely grated, plus Parmesan shavings to garnish

Make it now!

Preheat the oven to 160°C/325°F/Gas Mark 3. Put the tomatoes in a roasting tin, cut side up, sprinkle with the garlic and 2 tablespoons of olive oil and season well with salt and pepper. Roast for 40—45 minutes, or until softened and just beginning to brown. Leave to cool, then chop up any larger ones.

Meanwhile, put the pasta in a large saucepan of boiling water. Bring back to the boil, cover and simmer according to the packet instructions, until just tender. Drain into a colander, rinse with cold water, then drain again.

To make the pesto, put all the ingredients in a blender, add 25 g/1 oz baby spinach and the remaining 4 tablespoons of olive oil and whizz until smooth. Season lightly with salt and pepper.

Put the pasta and pesto in a salad bowl, toss together, then add the remaining spinach and toss again briefly. Add the tomatoes and any pan juices and toss gently. Garnish with the Parmesan shavings and basil leaves and serve.

Carbs for athletes

Athletes need 5—10 g of carbohydrate per kilogram of body weight each day, compared to the average person who needs 3—5 g. A portion of this salad provides 43 g of carbohydrate.

Pear, celery, blue cheese & walnut salad

Per serving: 382 cals 30.8g fat 7g sat fat 9.2g protein 17g carbs 6.5g fibre

Walnuts have long been revered as a healthy ingredient. In this autumn salad they combine with the blue cheese to give your body a boost.

Serves 4

* 2 large, juicy red-skinned pears
* 4 celery sticks, finely chopped
* squeeze of lemon juice
* 3 tbsp roughly chopped fresh flat-leaf parsley
* 150 g/5½ oz dark green salad leaves, such as rocket, watercress and baby spinach
* 100 g/3½ oz blue cheese, broken into small chunks
* 4 tbsp roughly chopped walnuts
* sea salt flakes

Dressing

* 1 tbsp lemon juice
* 4 tbsp walnut oil
* ¼ tsp pepper

Crunch time

Quarter and core one of the pears but do not peel it. Slice each quarter lengthways into thin segments. Put them in a salad bowl, add the celery and sprinkle over the lemon juice to prevent discolouration.

To make the dressing, quarter and core the second pear. Slice one quarter lengthways into thin segments and add to the bowl. Peel and roughly chop the remaining quarters and put them in a blender.

Put the remaining dressing ingredients in the blender and whizz until very smooth.

Add 5 tablespoons of the dressing, or just enough to coat, to the salad bowl. Stir in the parsley and season with a pinch of sea salt.

Arrange the salad leaves on four plates. Pile the pear and celery mixture on top. Sprinkle with the cheese and walnuts and serve immediately.

Go nuts for walnuts!

Walnuts are rich in monounsaturated fats and are a good source of omega-3 fatty acids. Eating 25 g/1 oz walnuts per day provides about 75 per cent of the omega-3 fatty acids we need.

Tomato & mozzarella superfood salad

Per serving: 377 cals   32g fat   7.3g sat fats   11.8g protein   14g carbs   7g fibre

Super-speedy to put together, this popular salad includes energy-boosting avocado, which is rich in monounsaturated healthy fats and antioxidant vitamins, and has more protein than any other fruit.

Serves 4

* 600 g/1lb 5 oz beef tomatoes, cut into thick wedges
* 150 g/5½ oz mozzarella cheese, drained and torn into pieces
* 2 avocados, halved, pitted, peeled and cut into slices
* few fresh basil leaves, torn
* 20 black olives, stoned

Dressing

* 4 tbsp olive oil
* 1½ tbsp white wine vinegar
* 1 tsp wholegrain mustard
* salt and pepper

Mix it up

Arrange the tomatoes, mozzarella and avocados in a large serving dish.

To make the dressing, put the oil, vinegar and mustard in a small bowl, mix together and season to taste with salt and pepper. Drizzle over the salad. Scatter the basil and olives on top and toss gently together. Serve immediately.

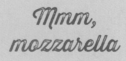

Mmm, mozzarella

Mozzarella is a good source of protein and calcium, for building strong, healthy teeth and bones. It is also high in fat, so will give you an energy boost, but should be eaten in moderation.

Avocados

This superfood is thought to be the most nutritionally complete fruit in the world. Containing numerous vitamins and minerals, phytonutrients and protein, it is a quick, simple nutrient- and energy-booster. The avocado does contain fat, which bumps up its calories – but it is monounsaturated fat, the good kind, which helps maintain healthy cholesterol levels and provides essential fatty acids. Plus they contain lutein, a natural antioxidant, which is thought to help maintain healthy eyesight and prevent macular degeneration as we age.

High-energy warm egg salad

Per serving: 365 cals   25.2g fat   4.3g sat fat   15.5g protein   21g carbs   5.8g fibre

For all those who say salads aren't filling, this one will prove you wrong! Packed with energy-boosting complex carbs, protein, vitamins and minerals, this summery lunch will super-power you through the afternoon.

Serves 4

Tapenade

* 425 g/15 oz broad beans, podded (175 g/6 oz podded weight)
* 55 g/2 oz green olives, stoned
* 25 g/1 oz fresh flat-leaf parsley, roughly chopped
* 40 g/1½ oz rocket
* 1 small garlic clove, thinly sliced

Salad

* 85 g/3 oz baby spinach
* 85 g/3 oz button mushrooms, sliced
* 1 tsp white wine vinegar
* 4 eggs
* 4 slices of rustic wholemeal bread
* salt and pepper

Dressing

* 4 tsp balsamic vinegar
* 4 tbsp light olive oil, plus extra to serve

How to make it

To make the tapenade, boil the broad beans in a saucepan of water for 5 minutes. Drain and transfer to a food processor. Add the olives, parsley, rocket and garlic and season with salt and pepper. Process until finely chopped, then keep warm.

Put the spinach and mushrooms in a salad bowl.

To make the dressing, put the vinegar and oil in a bowl, mix together and season with a little salt and pepper. Drizzle over the salad and toss gently together. Spoon the salad on to four plates.

Bring a wide saucepan of water to the boil. Add the white wine vinegar and a little salt, then stir and crack in the eggs one at a time. Simmer very gently, until the egg whites are just set but the yolks are still runny.

Meanwhile, toast the bread. Spread the tapenade over the toast and nestle each slice in the salad. Lift the eggs out of the water using a slotted spoon, then place on top of the toasts. Season with a little extra salt and pepper and sprinkle with a drizzle of olive oil, then serve immediately.

Broad bean-tastic

Broad beans are rich in complex carbohydrates for slow-release energy and soluble fibre. Although fibre does not contain energy or nutrients, it aids digestion and absorption of other foods and encourages healthy bowel movement, so may help to reduce symptoms of IBS and lower blood cholesterol.

Lovely & light avocado & almond salad

Per serving: 312 cals 25.7g fat 3.1g sat fat 7.4g protein 19.2g carbs 10.5g fibre

Smooth and tasty avocados are flavoured with zesty lemon juice, fragrant coriander, piquant spring onions and hot chilli, and given an added crunch with a sprinkling of flaked almonds!

Serves 4

* 2 tsp olive oil
* 55 g/2 oz flaked almonds
* 1 iceberg lettuce, quartered and torn into bite-sized pieces
* 3 avocados, halved, pitted and peeled
* juice of 2 lemons

Dressing

* 4 tbsp low-fat natural yogurt
* 2 spring onions, finely chopped
* ¼ tsp dried crushed red chillies
* 25 g/1 oz fresh coriander, finely chopped (optional)
* salt and pepper

Amazing almonds

Adding just a spoonful or two of almonds to a salad will help to boost its vitamin E, calcium and protein levels, and is especially beneficial for vegetarians.

Time to get started

Heat the oil in a frying pan over a medium heat. Add the almonds and cook for 3–4 minutes, or until golden, stirring often, then leave to cool.

Put the lettuce in a salad bowl. Slice two of the avocados, put them in a bowl and squeeze over the juice of 1½ lemons to prevent discolouration. Transfer them to the salad bowl.

To make the dressing, mash the remaining avocado on a plate with the remaining lemon juice. Mix in the yogurt, spring onions, dried chillies and coriander, if using, and season lightly with salt and pepper.

Spoon the salad into four shallow bowls, sprinkle with the cooked almonds, then spoon the dressing over the salad.

High-energy
warm egg salad
page 72

Lovely & light
avocado
& almond salad
page 73

Slow-release celeriac remoulade with asparagus

Remoulade dressing is classically made with mayonnaise and flavoured with mustard, gherkins and herbs. For a modern twist, low-fat natural yogurt has been mixed into the dressing to minimise the fat content.

Serves 4

* 450 g/1 lb celeriac, peeled and cut into matchsticks
* 450 g/1 lb potatoes, peeled and cut into matchsticks
* 55 g/2 oz walnut pieces, roughly chopped
* 55 g/2 oz gherkins, drained and chopped
* 4 tbsp finely snipped fresh chives
* 300 g/10½ oz asparagus, trimmed
* 2 tbsp olive oil
* salt and pepper

Dressing

* 3 tbsp light mayonnaise
* 3 tbsp low-fat natural yogurt
* 2 tsp Dijon mustard

Crunch time

Put the celeriac and potatoes in a saucepan of boiling water. Bring back to the boil, cover and simmer for 3–4 minutes, or until tender but still firm. Drain into a colander, rinse with cold water several times to cool quickly, then drain again and transfer to a bowl.

To make the dressing, put the mayonnaise and yogurt in a small bowl. Stir in the mustard and season well with salt and pepper. Pour over the celeriac and potatoes and toss gently together.

Mix in the walnuts, gherkins and chives. Divide between four shallow bowls.

Preheat a griddle pan or frying pan over a high heat. Put the asparagus and oil in a bowl, season well with salt and pepper and toss gently together. Cook in the hot pan for 3–4 minutes, or until just tender. Arrange over the salad and serve immediately.

Per serving: 353 cals   19.5g fat   2.2g sat fat   8.3g protein   40.3g carbs   6.9g fibre

Roasted beetroot & squash salad

Per serving: 505 cals   19.3g fat   2.5g sat fat   10g protein   75g carbs   9g fibre

This nutty-tasting wholegrain salad, topped with vibrant roast beetroot and butternut squash, can be made the night before, chilled, then tossed with the beetroot leaves just before you serve it. That means it's perfect for a power-boosting packed lunch!

Serves 4

* 450 g/1 lb raw beetroot, green stalk trimmed, peeled and cut into 2-cm/¾-inch cubes
* 450 g/1 lb butternut squash flesh, cut into 2-cm/¾-inch cubes
* 4 tbsp olive oil
* 100 g/3½ oz brown basmati rice
* 100 g/3½ oz red Camargue rice
* 100 g/3½ oz quick-cook farro
* 115 g/4 oz beetroot leaves
* salt and pepper

Dressing

* 1 tbsp flaxseed (linseed) oil
* 2 tbsp red wine vinegar
* ½ tsp smoked hot paprika
* 1 tsp fennel seeds, roughly crushed
* 2 tsp tomato purée

How to make it

Preheat the oven to 200°C/400°F/Gas Mark 6. Put the beetroot and squash in a roasting tin, drizzle with half the olive oil and season with a little salt and pepper. Roast for 30 minutes, or until just tender.

Meanwhile, put the basmati and red Camargue rice in a saucepan of boiling water. Bring back to the boil, then simmer, uncovered, for 15 minutes. Add the farro and cook for 10 minutes more, or until all the grains are tender. Drain and rinse, then transfer to a platter.

To make the dressing, put all the ingredients and the remaining 2 tablespoons of olive oil in a jam jar, season to taste with salt and pepper, screw on the lid and shake well. Drizzle over the rice mixture, then toss gently together.

Spoon the roasted vegetables over the grains and leave to cool. Toss gently together then sprinkle with the beetroot leaves and serve immediately.

The brighter the better

The brighter the butternut squash flesh, the more beta carotene it contains. This is converted into vitamin A, which is vital for healthy eyesight.

Three-bean energy-booster salad

Per serving: 276 cals 13.3g fat 1.6g sat fat 11g protein 29.6g carbs 11.4g fibre

This mighty salad will give you a slow, sustained energy boost. It is made with low-GI foods that are rich in fibre and carbohydrate and take time for the body to break down.

Serves 4

* 200 g/7 oz green beans, halved
* 200 g/7 oz frozen edamame beans or frozen broad beans
* 150 g/5½ oz frozen sweetcorn
* 400 g/14 oz canned red kidney beans, drained and rinsed
* 2 tbsp chia seeds

Dressing

* 3 tbsp olive oil
* 1 tbsp red wine vinegar
* 1 tsp wholegrain mustard
* 1 tsp agave syrup
* 4 tsp finely chopped fresh tarragon
* salt and pepper

Full of beans

Put the green beans, edamame beans and sweetcorn in a saucepan of boiling water. Bring back to the boil, then simmer for 4 minutes, until the green beans are just tender. Drain into a colander, rinse with cold water, then drain again and put into a salad bowl.

Add the kidney beans and chia seeds to the bowl and toss gently together.

To make the dressing, put the oil, vinegar and mustard in a jam jar, then add the agave syrup and tarragon and season to taste with salt and pepper. Screw on the lid and shake well. Drizzle over the salad, toss gently together and serve immediately.

Three cheers for chia

Originally eaten by the Mayans and Aztecs, chia seeds are rich in protein, which helps to build and repair muscles. They are the richest combined plant source of omega-3, -6 and -9 fatty acids. A tablespoon of chia seeds provides 5 g of fibre; women should aim for 25 g of fibre per day and a man 38 g.

Chunky avocado & sweetcorn salad

Per serving: 188 cals   12.5g fat   1.7g sat fat   3.3g protein   19.6g carbs   4.9g fibre

A light-tasting mix of creamy avocado, crunchy peppers, sweetcorn and kale flavoured with fresh coriander and tangy lime for a concentrated energy boost to see you through a busy afternoon.

Serves 4

* 200 g/7 oz frozen sweetcorn
* 1 large avocado, halved, pitted, peeled and cut into cubes
* 175 g/6 oz cherry tomatoes, cut into quarters
* ½ red onion, finely chopped
* 1 small green pepper, halved, deseeded and cut into small chunks
* 40 g/1½ oz kale, shredded
* 25 g/1 oz fresh coriander, roughly chopped

Dressing

* finely grated rind and juice of 1 lime
* 2 tbsp olive oil
* salt and pepper

How to make it

Put the sweetcorn in a saucepan of boiling water. Bring back to the boil, then simmer for 3 minutes. Drain into a colander, rinse with cold water, drain again, then transfer to a salad bowl.

To make the dressing, put the lime rind and juice and oil in a jam jar, season to taste with salt and pepper, screw on the lid and shake well.

Add the avocado, tomatoes, onion, green pepper, kale and coriander to the salad bowl. Drizzle over the dressing and toss together. Spoon into four bowls and serve immediately.

Sweet sweetcorn

Naturally sweet and packed with complex carbs and fibre, sweetcorn provides a sustained and stable energy boost to help us avoid mood swings.

Health

High-fibre chicken salad

Per serving: 694 cals 20g fat 3.2g sat fat 46.3g protein 79.7g carbs 5.6g fibre

Capture the flavours and colours of Morocco with this spicy brown rice salad flecked with jewel-like diced dried apricots and glistening raisins, and tossed with health-boosting green kale.

Serves 4

* 250 g/9 oz easy-cook brown rice
* 2 tsp tomato purée
* 500 g/1 lb 2 oz skinless chicken breast fillets
* 85 g/3 oz ready-to-eat dried apricots, diced
* 55 g/2 oz raisins
* 55 g/2 oz pickled lemons, drained and finely chopped
* 1 small red onion, finely chopped
* 85 g/3 oz kale, shredded
* 3 tbsp pine nuts, toasted

Dressing

* 2 tsp harissa
* 4 tbsp olive oil
* juice of 1 lemon
* salt and pepper

How to make it

Put the rice in a saucepan of boiling water. Bring back to the boil, then simmer for 25–30 minutes, or until tender. Drain, then transfer to a salad bowl.

Meanwhile, to make the dressing, put the harissa, oil and lemon juice in a jam jar, season to taste with salt and pepper, screw on the lid and shake well.

Spoon 2 tablespoons of the dressing into a bowl and mix in the tomato purée. Preheat the grill to high and line the grill pan with foil. Put the chicken on the foil in a single layer. Brush some of the tomato dressing over the chicken, then grill for 15–18 minutes, or until golden and cooked through, turning the meat and brushing it with the remaining tomato dressing halfway through cooking. Cut through the middle of a breast to check that the meat is no longer pink and any juices run clear and are piping hot. Cover and leave to cool.

Drizzle the remaining dressing over the rice in the salad bowl. Add the dried apricots, raisins, pickled lemons and onion, then toss gently together and leave to cool.

Add the kale and pine nuts to the salad and stir well. Thinly slice the chicken, arrange it over the salad and serve.

Health-giving rice

Rice is an important source of protein and energy. Easy-cook brown rice has a little of the bran removed and is parboiled before milling, speeding up cooking but retaining far more of the vital nutrients and fibre than white rice. Homeopaths believe that rice can help treat digestive disorders, from indigestion to diverticulitis.

Brain-boosting ruby couscous salad with griddled chicken

Per serving: 521 cals   16.5g fat   2g sat fat   45.8g protein   48.4g carbs   5.2g fibre

This salad looks good and does you good too! The beetroot turns everything a deep vibrant red and glistens jewel-like with the pomegranate seeds.

Serves 4

* 175 g/6 oz giant wholewheat couscous
* 175 g/6 oz cooked beetroot, in natural juices (drained weight), drained and diced
* 1 small red onion, finely chopped
* 125 g/4½ oz cherry tomatoes, halved
* 1 pomegranate, halved and seeds removed and reserved
* juice of 2 lemons
* 2 tbsp flaxseed (linseed) oil
* 2 tbsp olive oil
* 4 tsp tomato purée
* 2 tbsp roughly chopped fresh mint
* 1 tsp black peppercorns, roughly crushed
* 500 g/1 lb 2 oz chicken breast mini fillets, sliced
* salt and pepper

Create your salad

Put the couscous in a saucepan of boiling water. Bring back to the boil, then simmer for 6–8 minutes, or until just tender. Drain into a sieve, rinse with cold water, then transfer to a salad bowl. Add the beetroot, then the onion, tomatoes and pomegranate seeds.

To make the dressing, put the juice of one lemon, the flaxseed oil, half the olive oil and half the tomato purée in a jam jar, season to taste with salt and pepper, screw on the lid and shake well. Drizzle over the salad, then sprinkle on the chopped mint and toss together.

Put the remaining lemon juice, olive oil and tomato purée and the crushed peppercorns in a clean plastic bag, twist and shake well. Add the chicken, seal, then shake until the chicken is evenly coated.

Preheat a ridged griddle pan over a high heat. Cook the chicken (in batches if necessary) in the hot pan for 10 minutes, turning once or twice, until cooked through. Cut through the middle of a slice to check that the meat is no longer pink and any juices run clear and are piping hot. Arrange over the salad and serve.

Brain-boosting beetroot

The high levels of nitrates in beetroot may help slow down the progression of dementia. When the pigment betacyanin, which gives beetroot its colour, combines with carotenoids and flavonoids, it may help reduce the oxidation of LDL cholesterol, so protecting artery walls and reducing the risk of heart disease and stroke.

Pick-me-up prawn & white bean salad

Per serving: 408 cals   19.5g fat   3.1g sat fat   23.5g protein   35g carbs   3.4g fibre

Forget about student-style beans on toast! This stylish version mixes canned haricot beans with prawns in a tangy lemon and parsley dressing for a fresh-tasting, protein-boosting, salad-style alternative.

Serves 4

* 400 g/14 oz canned haricot beans, drained and rinsed
* ½ red onion, finely chopped
* 1 celery stick, finely chopped
* 300 g/10½ oz cooked, large peeled prawns with tails intact, thawed if frozen
* 1 garlic clove, finely chopped
* juice of 1 lemon
* 5 tbsp extra virgin olive oil
* 2 tbsp roughly chopped fresh flat-leaf parsley, plus 15 g/½ oz fresh flat-leaf parsley leaves, to garnish
* 4 thick slices of country bread (pain de campagne)
* 85 g/3 oz baby plum tomatoes, halved
* salt and pepper

Crunch time

Put the beans, onion, celery, prawns and garlic in a large shallow bowl. Add the lemon juice, 2 tablespoons of the oil and the parsley. Season lightly with salt and pepper, stir well, then cover and set aside.

Preheat a ridged griddle pan over a high heat. Brush the bread with some of the remaining oil. Cook in the hot pan for 2–3 minutes on each side, or until golden. Transfer to four plates.

Gently stir the tomatoes into the salad. Pile the salad on to the hot toasts. Drizzle over the rest of the olive oil, garnish with the parsley leaves, season with a little more pepper and serve.

The power of white beans

White beans offer extraordinary health benefits. They are loaded with antioxidants and provide a good supply of detoxifying molybdenum. They are also a good source of fibre and protein and rank low on the glycaemic index. They produce alpha-amylase inhibitors, which help regulate fat storage in the body.

Vitamin B-boosting feta, mint & strawberry salad

Per serving: 354 cals 30g fat 12g sat fat 11.3g protein 12g carbs 3.2g fibre

Strawberries are a great way to boost your vitamin C, which is needed daily by the body. Their natural sweetness works well with the saltiness of the feta cheese and crispness of the blanched beans in this salad.

Serves 4

* 250 g/9 oz green beans
* 250 g/9 oz strawberries, hulled and halved
* 1 tbsp shelled pistachio nuts
* 15 g/½ oz fresh mint
* 250 g/9 oz feta cheese (drained weight), broken into chunks
* pepper

Dressing

* 1 tbsp raspberry vinegar
* 1 tsp agave syrup
* 1 tsp Dijon mustard
* 3 tbsp olive oil
* salt

For your salad

To make the dressing, put the vinegar, agave syrup, mustard and a pinch of salt in a bowl and stir until smooth. Slowly pour in the oil, whisking constantly.

Put the beans in a saucepan of boiling water. Bring back to the boil, then simmer for 5 minutes, or until just tender. Drain into a colander, rinse with cold water, then drain again and put into a salad bowl. Add the strawberries, pistachio nuts and mint. Drizzle over enough dressing to coat lightly, then toss gently together.

Scatter the feta over the salad, season well with pepper and serve immediately.

Super strawberries

Strawberries have more vitamin C than any other red berries and so have good antiviral and antibacterial properties. They are rich in beta carotene. Their natural fruit sugars also give the body an energy boost.

Ratatouille & bean salad

Per serving: 167.5 cals   4.6g fat   0.6g sat fat   8.4g protein   23g carbs   9g fibre

This healthy, high-fibre salad can be eaten slightly warm and then any leftovers refrigerated and taken to work the next day in a lunchbox, with the leaves in a separate plastic bag to keep them fresh.

Serves 4

* 1 tbsp olive oil
* 1 red onion, roughly chopped
* 1 red pepper, halved, deseeded and cut into chunks
* 1 green pepper, halved, deseeded and cut into chunks
* 1 orange pepper, halved, deseeded and cut into chunks
* 2 garlic cloves, finely chopped
* 350 g/12 oz tomatoes, skinned and roughly chopped
* 1 tbsp tomato purée
* ¼ tsp smoked hot paprika
* 2 stems of fresh rosemary
* 2 courgettes, cut into chunks
* 400 g/14 oz canned cannellini beans, drained and rinsed
* 55 g/2 oz mixed baby salad leaves, including red chard, mustard leaves and rocket or mizuna
* 1 tbsp balsamic vinegar
* salt and pepper

Mix it up

Heat the oil in a saucepan over a medium heat. Add the onion and fry gently for 5 minutes, stirring, until softened and just beginning to brown. Add the peppers, garlic and tomatoes, then stir in the tomato purée and paprika.

Add the rosemary and season well with salt and pepper. Cover and simmer for 10 minutes. Stir in the courgettes and cook for 5 minutes, until just beginning to soften but still bright green.

Remove the pan from the heat and stir in the cannellini beans. Season to taste with salt and pepper and discard the rosemary. Transfer to a salad bowl and leave to cool.

When ready to serve, toss the baby leaves in the balsamic vinegar and scatter over the salad. Serve in shallow bowls.

Beetroot, spinach & Brie nutrient-boosting salad

Per serving: 459 cals 39.8g fat 12g sat fat 15g protein 14g carbs 4.1g fibre

Packed with vitamins and minerals, this vibrant salad is topped with meltingly soft Brie and toasted walnuts, and is so delicious you'll be coming back for more.

Serves 4

* 175 g/6 oz baby spinach
* 175 g/6 oz raw beetroot, green stalk trimmed, peeled and very thinly sliced
* 115 g/4 oz ready-to-eat sprouting mung bean mix
* 175 g/6 oz Brie, diced

Dressing

* 85 g/3 oz walnut pieces
* 1 tsp fennel seeds, roughly crushed
* 4 tbsp rice bran oil
* 2 tbsp red wine vinegar
* 2 tsp brown rice syrup
* salt and pepper

Give it a whirl

Put the spinach, beetroot and sprouting mung bean mix in a salad bowl.

To make the dressing, preheat a frying pan over a medium heat. Put the walnuts and fennel seeds in the hot pan and cook for 2–3 minutes, until lightly toasted. Remove from the heat and add the rice bran oil, then leave to cool for 5 minutes.

Strain the cooled oil into a jam jar, add the vinegar and rice syrup and season to taste with salt and pepper. Screw on the lid and shake well. Drizzle over the salad and toss gently together.

Scatter the Brie over the salad and spoon the walnuts and fennel on top. Serve immediately.

Health benefits of Brie

There's no getting away from the fact that Brie contains fat, but the fat content is surprisingly lower than that of hard cheeses such as Gruyère or Cheddar, even though Brie looks so soft and creamy. Compare 28 g of fat, of which 17.4 g is saturated fat, per 100 g of Brie to 33 g of fat, of which 19 g is saturated fat, per 100 g for mature Gruyère.

Ratatouille &
bean salad

page 92

Beetroot,
spinach & Brie
nutrient-boosting
salad

page 93

Fattoush

This brightly coloured Lebanese salad is packed with the fresh taste of lemon, mint and coriander and topped with warm pieces of griddled pitta bread.

Serves 4

* 1 small red pepper, halved, deseeded and diced
* 1 small yellow pepper, halved, deseeded and diced
* 1 small green pepper, halved, deseeded and diced
* 300 g/10½ oz cucumber, peeled, halved lengthways, deseeded and diced
* 2 spring onions, finely chopped
* 25 g/1 oz fresh mint, finely chopped
* 25 g/1 oz fresh coriander, finely chopped
* 2 pitta breads
* 85 g/3 oz feta cheese (drained weight), crumbled

Dressing

* juice of 1 lemon
* 3 tbsp olive oil
* ½ tsp cumin seeds, roughly crushed
* 1 garlic clove, finely chopped
* pepper

How to make it

Put the peppers, cucumber and spring onions in a salad bowl, sprinkle over the herbs and toss gently together.

To make the dressing, put the lemon juice, oil, cumin and garlic in a jam jar, season with a little pepper, screw on the lid and shake well. Drizzle over the salad and toss gently together, then spoon into four bowls.

Preheat a griddle pan over a medium heat. Cook the pitta breads in the hot pan for 1½ minutes on each side, until hot and puffy. Transfer to a plate and cut into small pieces. Sprinkle the pitta and feta over the salad and serve immediately.

Per serving: 263 cals   15.3g fat   4.7g sat fat   7.2g protein   25g carbs   3.3g fibre

High-fibre Green lentil salad

Per serving: 429 cals 17.6g fat 4.2g sat fat 23.5g protein 44.6g carbs 6.9g fibre

Salads needn't only be enjoyed when the weather is hot. This robust, earthy lentil salad can be rustled up quickly after work and, as it is served just-warm, makes a great dish for cooler autumn days.

Serves 4

* 850 ml/1½ pints vegetable stock
* 2 bay leaves
* 1 cinnamon stick, halved
* 225 g/8 oz leeks
* 225 g/8 oz green lentils, rinsed and drained
* 3 tbsp olive oil
* 2 garlic cloves, finely chopped
* 4 eggs
* 2 tbsp capers, drained and chopped
* 85 g/3 oz baby spinach
* 25 g/1 oz fresh flat-leaf parsley, roughly chopped

Dressing

* 2 tbsp red wine vinegar
* 1 tsp Dijon mustard
* salt and pepper

Toss it together

Put the stock, bay and cinnamon in a saucepan and bring just to the boil. Cut a 7.5-cm/3-inch piece from the white base of one of the leeks and add this and the lentils to the pan. Cover and simmer for 25 minutes, or until the lentils are tender and nearly all the stock has been absorbed. Top up with a little boiling water during cooking if needed. Drain the lentils, transfer to a salad bowl and discard the cooked leek, bay leaves and cinnamon stick.

Meanwhile, thinly slice the rest of the leeks. Heat 1 tablespoon of olive oil in a frying pan over a medium heat. Add the sliced leeks and the garlic and fry for 3–4 minutes, stirring, until just beginning to soften. Remove from the heat and leave to cool.

Put the eggs in a saucepan and pour in enough cold water to cover them by 1 cm/½ inch. Bring to the boil, then reduce the heat and boil for 8 minutes. Drain immediately, cool quickly under cold running water, then peel and cut into quarters.

To make the dressing, put the vinegar, remaining 2 tablespoons of oil and the mustard in a jam jar, season to taste with salt and pepper, screw on the lid and shake well. Drizzle over the lentils and toss gently together. Top with the sliced leeks, capers and spinach. Arrange the hard-boiled eggs over the salad, sprinkle with the parsley and serve warm.

Oh-so-good-for-you purple sprouting broccoli salad

Per serving: 232 cals   11.1g fat   1.4g sat fat   6.2g protein   29g carbs   6.5g fibre

Broccoli is one of the main superfoods. It contains sulforaphane, which is thought to have a powerful anti-cancer effect, especially against tumours of the digestive tract, lungs and prostrate gland. Steam broccoli where possible, as boiling halves the amount of vitamin C it contains.

Serves 4

* 200 g/7 oz purple sprouting broccoli
* 250 g/9 oz red cabbage, shredded
* 115 g/4 oz cooked beetroot in natural juices (drained weight), drained and cut into matchsticks
* 2 tbsp dried cranberries
* 3 tbsp balsamic vinegar

Croutons

* 2 tbsp olive oil
* 85 g/3 oz rustic wholegrain bread, torn into small pieces
* 1 tbsp sunflower seeds
* 1 tbsp flaxseeds (linseeds)

Crunch time

Put the broccoli in the top of a steamer, cover and set over a saucepan of simmering water. Steam for 3–5 minutes, or until tender. Cool under cold running water, then cut the stems in half and the lower stems in half again lengthways, and transfer them to a salad bowl.

Add the red cabbage, beetroot and dried cranberries to the salad bowl.

To make the croütons, heat the oil in a frying pan over a medium heat, add the bread and fry for 3–4 minutes, stirring, until just beginning to brown. Add the sunflower seeds and flaxseeds and cook for 2–3 minutes more, until lightly toasted.

Drizzle the balsamic vinegar over the salad and toss gently together. Sprinkle with the croutons and seeds and serve.

Go to the dark side...

The darker the broccoli florets, either purple, green or deep blue-green, the higher the amount of beta carotene and vitamin C. It also contains folates, iron and potassium.

Mineral-boosting three-seed salad

Per serving: 212 cals 14.6g fat 2g sat fat 6.7g protein 16g carbs 4.7g fibre

Protein- and mineral-rich seeds are blended with yogurt and lemon for a hummus-style dressing that tastes delicious over spinach and celery leaves.

Serves 4

* 115 g/4 oz baby spinach
* ½ oakleaf lettuce, leaves separated and torn into bite-sized pieces
* 2 celery sticks, sliced
* small handful of celery leaves, roughly chopped, plus a few extra to garnish
* 150 g/5½ oz blueberries
* juice of 2 lemons
* salt and pepper

Dressing

* 2 tbsp sesame seeds, toasted, plus a few extra to garnish
* 2 tbsp sunflower seeds
* 2 tbsp flaxseeds (linseeds)
* 1 garlic clove, sliced
* 2 tbsp olive oil
* 150 g/5½ oz low-fat natural yogurt

How to make it

Put the spinach and lettuce in a salad bowl. Sprinkle over the celery, celery leaves and blueberries. Drizzle over the juice of one lemon, season with a little salt and pepper and toss gently together.

To make the dressing, put the sesame seeds, sunflower seeds and flaxseeds in a blender. Add the garlic, oil and juice of the remaining lemon and season to taste with salt and pepper. Whizz until the seeds are finely ground, then scrape down the sides of the goblet and add the yogurt. Whizz again briefly until you have a fine paste.

Divide the salad between four plates and add a generous spoonful of the dressing to the centre of each plate. Garnish with a few extra sesame seeds and celery leaves and serve.

Seeds of good health

Flaxseeds (linseeds) have the most minerals of all the seeds, containing calcium, magnesium, phosphorus, potassium and zinc. If they are eaten whole they tend not to be absorbed by the body, but if they are blended they are well absorbed. Sunflower and sesame seeds are good sources of vitamin E, and sesame seeds also contain calcium. All the seeds contain protein and fibre and are high in unsaturated fats.

Protective Indian spiced slaw

Per serving: 193 cals   12g fat   1.6g sat fat   7.2g protein   17g carbs   4.2g fibre

Forget about mayonnaise, this extra-healthy coleslaw is made with low-fat natural yogurt instead, then spiced with garam masala and turmeric for an exotic twist.

Serves 4

* 150 g/5½ oz low-fat natural yogurt
* 175 g/6 oz red cabbage, shredded
* 40 g/1½ oz kale, shredded
* 1 red apple, cored and coarsely grated
* 1 large carrot, coarsely grated
* salt and pepper

Topping

* 2 tbsp pumpkin seeds
* 2 tbsp sunflower seeds
* 2 tbsp flaked almonds
* 1½ tsp garam masala
* ½ tsp turmeric
* 1 tbsp sunflower oil

Mix it up

To make the topping, preheat a frying pan over a medium heat. Put the pumpkin seeds, sunflower seeds, almonds, ½ teaspoon of garam masala and ¼ teaspoon of turmeric in the hot pan and pour on the oil. Cook for 3—4 minutes, stirring often, until the almonds are golden brown. Leave to cool.

To make the dressing, put the yogurt and remaining 1 teaspoon of garam masala and ¼ teaspoon of turmeric in a large bowl, then season to taste with salt and pepper and stir well.

Add the cabbage, kale, apple and carrot to the bowl and toss gently together. Divide the salad between four bowls, sprinkle on the topping and serve.

Boost your immunity

Red cabbage, kale and carrots are all high in antioxidants, and the vitamin C-rich apples will help boost your immune system.

Immune-boosting summer veg carpaccio

Per serving: 359 cals 21.4g fat 2.8g sat fat 8.8g protein 36.8g carbs 10.6g fibre

The secret of this pretty, vibrant-coloured salad is to cut the vegetables as thinly as possible so that you can almost see through the slices. A mandolin is perfect for this, but do mind your fingers. If you don't have one, your favourite knife will work equally well, but will take a little longer.

Serves 4

Hummus

* 400 g/14 oz canned chickpeas, drained and rinsed
* 1 garlic clove, finely chopped
* 1 tbsp chia seeds
* 2 tbsp sesame seeds, toasted
* juice of 1 lemon
* 2 tbsp olive oil
* salt and pepper

Salad

* 300 g/10½ oz asparagus, thinly sliced lengthways
* 2 carrots, very thinly sliced lengthways
* 1 raw red beetroot, green stalk trimmed, peeled and very thinly sliced, any tiny leaves reserved
* 1 raw golden beetroot, green stalk trimmed, peeled and very thinly sliced, any tiny leaves reserved
* 85 g/3 oz yellow cherry tomatoes, thinly sliced
* 350 g/12 oz tomatoes, thinly sliced

Dressing

* juice of ½ lemon
* 3 tbsp olive oil
* 1 tsp Dijon mustard

Crunch time

To make the hummus, put the chickpeas, garlic, chia seeds and sesame seeds in a food processor. Add the lemon juice and oil and season well with salt and pepper. Whizz until you have a coarse, spreadable paste.

Put the asparagus, carrots, beetroots, yellow cherry tomatoes and salad tomatoes in a salad bowl.

To make the dressing, put the lemon juice, oil and mustard in a jam jar, season with a little salt and pepper, screw on the lid and shake well. Drizzle over the salad in the bowl and toss gently together.

To serve, spoon the hummus into the centre of four plates, then spread into a thin circle using the back of the spoon. Pile the salad on top, garnish with the reserved tiny beetroot leaves and serve.

Wheatberry & goji berry salad

Per serving: 420 cals 22.8g fat 3.1g sat fat 12.8g protein 49g carbs 10g fibre

Wheatberries are small, wholegrain wheat kernels with all the bran, germ and everything in-between. They are packed with complex carbohydrates, vitamin B, vitamin E, a range of minerals and fibre. With a great, nutty taste, they make a healthy alternative to rice in salads.

Serves 4

* 600 ml/1 pint vegetable stock
* 150 g/5½ oz wheatberries
* 40 g/1½ oz dried goji berries
* 2 carrots
* 115 g/4 oz kale, shredded

Dressing

* 55 g/2 oz hazelnuts, roughly chopped
* 2 tbsp sesame seeds
* 2 tbsp sunflower seeds
* 2 tbsp soy sauce
* 2 tbsp sesame oil
* juice of ½ orange

Time to get started

Bring the stock to the boil in a saucepan, add the wheatberries and simmer for 25 minutes, or until just tender. Drain off and discard the stock, spoon the wheatberries into a salad bowl and stir in the goji berries.

To make the dressing, dry-fry the hazelnuts, sesame seeds and sunflower seeds in a frying pan over a medium—high heat for 3—4 minutes, or until just turning golden brown. Remove from the heat, stir in the soy sauce, then leave to cool for 1 minute. Mix in the sesame oil and orange juice. Spoon half over the wheatberries, toss together, then leave to cool.

Shave the carrots into long, thin ribbons using a swivel-bladed vegetable peeler and add to the salad bowl. Add the kale, toss gently together, then spoon over the remaining dressing and serve.

Gorgeous goji berries

These tiny Himalayan red berries are rich in beta carotene and are a good source of B vitamins and antioxidants. Some people believe they may even help reduce cellulite!

Immune-
boosting summer
veg carpaccio

page 104

Wheatberry
& goji berry
salad

page 105

Spinach & tomato salad with roasted garlic croûtes

When it's roasted, garlic loses its pungency and has a mild, almost sweet flavour.

Serves 4

* 1 garlic bulb, halved crossways
* 6 tbsp olive oil
* 85 g/3 oz baby spinach
* 85 g/3 oz mixed salad leaves
* 225 g/8 oz cherry tomatoes, halved
* 4 slices of wholemeal French bread

Dressing

* 2 tbsp pumpkin seeds
* 2 tbsp sunflower seeds
* 2 tbsp flaxseeds (linseeds), roughly crushed
* ¼ tsp smoked hot paprika
* 4 tsp balsamic vinegar
* salt and pepper

Crunch time

Preheat the oven to 180°C/350°F/Gas Mark 4. Put the garlic halves into a piece of crumpled foil and place in a small roasting tin. Drizzle over 1 tablespoon of olive oil and roast for 20 minutes, or until the cloves are golden and softened.

To make the dressing, dry-fry the pumpkin seeds, sunflower seeds and flaxseeds in a frying pan over a medium–high heat for 3–4 minutes, or until just turning golden brown. Remove from the heat, stir in the smoked paprika and 4 tablespoons of olive oil, then leave to cool.

When the dressing is cool, add the balsamic vinegar and season to taste with salt and pepper.

Put the spinach and salad leaves in a salad bowl, then scatter over the tomatoes. Drizzle with the dressing and toss gently together, then divide between four plates.

Toast the bread on both sides. Scoop the soft garlic cloves from their papery casing, then very finely chop the flesh until you have a coarse paste. Spread thinly over the toasts and season with a little salt and pepper. Arrange on top of the salads, drizzle with the remaining olive oil and serve.

Per serving: 378 cals 29g fat 3.9g sat fat 7.9g protein 24.6g carbs 5g fibre

Three-berry bonanza

Per serving: 169 cals 10.8g fat 0.7g sat fat 2.2g protein 17g carbs 4g fibre

Serve this fresh fruit salad as a side dish or starter. The clean, tangy flavours will wake up your taste-buds and it will boost the health of your immune system.

Serves 4

* 1 small head of radicchio, leaves separated and torn into bite-sized pieces
* ½ oakleaf or brown-tinged lollo rosso lettuce, leaves separated and torn into bite-sized pieces
* 25 g/1 oz dried goji berries
* 115 g/4 oz raspberries
* 115 g/4 oz blueberries

Dressing

* 3 tbsp hemp oil
* juice of ½ lemon
* 1 tsp brown rice syrup
* salt and pepper

Hooray for hemp

Hemp oil contains more omega-3, -6 and -9 fatty acids (the good polyunsaturated fats) than any other oil used for cooking.

How to make it

Put the radicchio and oakleaf lettuce in a salad bowl. Add the goji berries, raspberries and blueberries and toss gently together.

To make the dressing, put the hemp oil, lemon juice and brown rice syrup in a jam jar, season with a little salt and pepper, screw on the lid and shake well. Drizzle over the salad and toss gently together. Spoon into four shallow bowls and serve.

Green goddess

Per serving: 250 cals   17.7g fat   2g sat fat   10g protein   11g carbs   6.5g fibre

A pretty, delicate salad from a summer garden. Garnish with a few tiny herb or viola flowers, or nasturtium or marigold petals if you wish.

Serves 4

* 200 g/7 oz frozen edamame beans, or podded broad beans
* 115 g/4 oz green beans
* 500 g/1 lb 2 oz peas in pods, any very tiny flat pods halved, the rest podded
* 50 g/1¾ oz pea shoots
* 50 g/1¾ oz ready-to-eat sprouting seeds, such as alfalfa and radish sprouts

Dressing

* 2 tbsp rice bran oil
* 2 tbsp olive oil
* juice of 1 lime
* 1 tsp agave syrup
* 2-cm/¾-inch piece of fresh ginger, peeled and finely grated
* salt and pepper

How to make it

Bring a saucepan of water to the boil, add the edamame beans and green beans and simmer for 2 minutes. Add any pea pods and simmer for 1 minute more. Drain into a sieve, cool under cold running water and drain again. Transfer to a salad bowl and sprinkle over the raw peas.

To make the dressing, put the rice bran oil, olive oil, lime juice, agave syrup and ginger in a jam jar, season with a little salt and pepper, screw on the lid and shake well.

Drizzle the dressing over the salad and toss gently together. Top with the pea shoots and sprouting seeds and serve immediately.

Perfect peas

Serving the peas raw means that you don't lose any vitamin C or thiamine content, a proportion of which is lost during cooking as these vitamins are water-soluble.

Sprouting seeds

Think of sprouting seeds, sometimes called salad sprouts, as a nutritional powerhouse. As the seeds germinate and begin to sprout, their natural nutrients multiply to meet the growing needs of the young shoots. This makes them a good way to add a range of antioxidants and immune-boosting vitamins, minerals and protein to a salad. As the seeds sprout, so the plant enzymes increase, which also aids digestion. Choose from alfalfa, adzuki, beetroot, broccoli or red clover seeds for a colourful, fresh-tasting, low-priced, all-year-round addition to any salad. Children younger than five, older adults, pregnant women and those with weakened immune systems are particularly vulnerable to the bacteria that may be present on sprouts and therefore should not eat raw sprouts and only eat sprouts that have been thoroughly cooked. Buy pre-packed sprouting seeds from the shops or grow them from a kit following the manufacturer's instructions, and wash them well before eating.

Cholesterol-lowering multi-grain salad

Per serving: 384 cals   17.6g fat   3g sat fat   9.8g protein   45g carbs   8g fibre

There is evidence that adding plenty of soluble fibre from grains or wholefoods, such as wild rice, bulgar wheat and quinoa, to the diet lowers blood cholesterol levels as the gum-like substance binds with cholesterol and carries it out of the body.

Serves 4

* 700 ml/1¼ pints vegetable stock
* 40 g/1½ oz wild rice
* 115 g/4 oz bulgar wheat
* 115 g/4 oz quinoa
* 2 courgettes, diagonally sliced
* 4 spring onions, halved lengthways
* 4 tbsp olive oil
* juice ½ lemon
* 1 tsp cumin seeds, roughly crushed
* 25 g/1 oz fresh flat-leaf parsley, roughly chopped
* 50 g/1¾ oz mixed ready-to-eat sprouting seeds, such as alfalfa and radish sprouts
* salt and pepper

Dressing

* finely grated rind and juice of ½ unwaxed lemon
* finely grated rind and juice of 1 lime
* 1 tsp runny honey

To make this salad

Bring the stock to the boil in a saucepan, add the rice and simmer for 5 minutes. Add the bulgar wheat and simmer for 5 minutes more. Add the quinoa and simmer for 10—12 minutes, or until all the grains are tender. Drain off and discard the stock and spoon the grains into a salad bowl.

To make the dressing, put the lemon and lime rind and juices, honey and 2 tablespoons of olive oil in a jam jar, season to taste with salt and pepper, screw on the lid and shake well. Drizzle over the grains, toss gently together, then leave to cool.

Meanwhile, mix the courgettes and onions with the remaining 2 tablespoons of olive oil, the lemon juice and cumin and season with a little salt and pepper.

Preheat a ridged griddle pan over a high heat. Cook the courgettes and onion in the hot pan for 1—2 minutes on each side, or until browned. Transfer to a plate and leave to cool. Serve the grains on four plates and top with the griddled vegetables. Garnish with the parsley and sprouting seeds and serve.

Fibre facts

Soluble dietary fibre stabilizes blood sugar levels by slowing down the rate at which glucose is absorbed by the body, so helping to avoid drops in energy and mood swings.

Slimming

Turkey & cranberry salad

Per serving: 327 cals 2.6g fat 0.6g sat fat 22.5g protein 53.3g carbs 4.2g fibre

Enjoy all the flavour of turkey, but in a salad! Why not take this to a bring-and-share supper, or pack individual portions for a work lunch — put the rocket in a separate bag and add just before serving so that it stays crisp.

Serves 4

* 150 g/5½ oz brown basmati rice
* 40 g/1½ oz wild rice
* 250 g/9 oz raw turkey breast slices
* 40 g/1½ oz dried cranberries
* 3 spring onions, finely chopped
* 200 g/7 oz tomatoes, diced
* 1 small red pepper, halved, deseeded and cut into chunks
* 55 g/2 oz rocket
* 40 g/1½ oz wafer-thin sliced lean ready-to-eat ham, cut into strips
* salt and pepper

Dressing

* 1½ tbsp cranberry sauce
* 1½ tbsp sherry vinegar
* finely grated rind and juice of 1 small unwaxed lemon
* 1 level tsp Dijon mustard

Toss it together

Put cold water in the base of a steamer, bring to the boil, then add the brown rice and wild rice and bring back to the boil. Put the turkey in the top of the steamer in a single layer, season with salt and pepper, then put it on the steamer base, cover and steam for 15 minutes, or until the turkey is cooked; cut into the middle of a slice to check that the meat is no longer pink and that the juices are clear and piping hot. Remove the steamer top and cook the rice for 5–10 minutes more, or until tender.

Dice the turkey and put it in a bowl. Add the cranberries. Drain and rinse the rice, then add to the bowl.

To make the dressing, put the cranberry sauce in a small saucepan and place over a low heat until just melted. Remove from the heat, then add the vinegar, lemon rind and juice, mustard and a little salt and pepper. Whisk together until smooth, then drizzle over the salad and leave to cool.

Add the spring onions, tomatoes and red pepper to the salad. Toss gently together, then divide between four plates. Top with the rocket and ham and serve.

Steak salad with light Thousand Island dressing

Per serving: 287 cals 8g fat 2.8g sat fat 35.7g protein 18.4g carbs 4.6g fibre

This salad is traditionally made with mayonnaise, but this light Thousand Island dressing tastes just as good. It's great with steak, or try it with cooked peeled prawns.

Serves 4

* 85 g/3 oz wholemeal seeded bread, cut into cubes
* little low-fat cooking spray
* 115 g/4 oz green beans, halved
* 150 g/5½ oz broccoli, cut into florets, stems sliced
* 2 x 250 g/9 oz sirloin steaks, all visible fat removed
* ½ iceberg lettuce, leaves separated and torn into bite-sized pieces
* 150 g/5½ oz cucumber, halved lengthways, deseeded and sliced

Dressing

* 200 g/7 oz low-fat natural yogurt
* 2 tsp tomato purée
* 2 tsp Worcestershire sauce
* ½ tsp powdered sweetener
* salt and pepper

Beef it up

Preheat the oven to 200°C/400°F/Gas Mark 6. Sprinkle the bread over a baking tray, spray with low-fat cooking spray and bake for 8–10 minutes, or until golden brown. Meanwhile, put the beans and broccoli in the top of a steamer, cover and set over a saucepan of simmering water. Steam for 3–5 minutes, or until tender. Cool under cold running water.

To make the dressing, put the yogurt, tomato purée, Worcestershire sauce and sweetener in a bowl, then season lightly with salt and pepper.

Preheat a griddle pan over a high heat. Spray the steaks with low-fat cooking spray, then season with salt and pepper. Cook in the hot pan for 2 minutes on each side for medium–rare, 3 minutes for medium and 4 minutes for well done. Transfer to a plate for a few minutes. Put the lettuce, cucumber and steamed vegetables in a bowl. Drizzle over the dressing and toss. Sprinkle with the croûtons. Divide the salad between four bowls. Thinly slice the steaks and arrange over the top, then serve.

Good bacteria

As fermented milk, yogurt is a natural source of probiotics, which help us to maintain a healthy gut and immune system. Research has shown that yogurt can even improve your cholesterol if eaten regularly.

Spiced chicken salad

Per serving: 257 cals   6.5g fat   1.5g sat fat   42g protein   7.5g carbs   1.5g fibre

This yogurt marinade, made with mellow Indian spices, is low in fat but full of flavour. Serve the chicken straight from the grill over the cool, crisp salad leaves for the best result.

Serves 4

* 85 g/3 oz mixed mustard leaves, such as red coral leaf, mustard and red mustard leaves
* 115 g/4 oz mixed lettuce leaves
* 150 g/5½ oz cucumber, very thinly sliced
* 25 g/1 oz fresh coriander, roughly chopped

Spiced chicken

* 200 g/7 oz low-fat natural yogurt
* 1 tsp cumin seeds, roughly crushed
* 1 tsp garam masala
* ½ tsp turmeric
* 1 garlic clove, finely chopped
* 2 tbsp finely chopped fresh coriander
* 500 g/1 lb 2 oz skinless chicken breast fillets, cut into cubes
* salt and pepper

Dressing

* 1 tbsp olive oil
* ½ tsp cumin seeds, roughly crushed
* ½ tsp dried crushed red chillies
* juice of 1 lemon
* ½ tsp powdered sweetener

Sizzle time!

To make the spiced chicken, spoon the yogurt into a bowl, add the cumin seeds, garam masala and turmeric, then the garlic and coriander, and season with a little salt and pepper. Stir, then add the chicken and toss gently together until the meat is evenly coated. Cover and chill in the fridge for 1 hour.

To make the dressing, put the oil in a frying pan, sprinkle on the cumin and crushed chillies and warm over a medium heat for 1–2 minutes, or until the aroma rises up. Remove from the heat, add the lemon juice, then stir in the sweetener and leave to cool.

When ready to serve, put the mustard and lettuce leaves in a salad bowl. Scatter the cucumber and coriander over the top. Preheat the grill to medium–hot. Thread the chicken on to eight metal skewers and grill, turning several times, for 12–15 minutes, or until browned and cooked through. Cut through the middle of a piece to check that the meat is no longer pink and any juices run clear and are piping hot. Drizzle the dressing over the salad. Slide the chicken off the skewers on to the salad.

Spiced chicken
salad

page 121

Steak salad with
light Thousand
Island dressing

page 120

Jerk turkey with tropical fruit salsa

Full of Caribbean flavour, this easy low-fat, low-calorie supper is really filling and satisfying!

Serves 4

* 1 butterhead lettuce, leaves separated and torn into bite-sized pieces
* juice of 1 lime
* 1 small pineapple, trimmed, peeled, quartered, cored and cut into thin wedges
* 450 g/1 lb raw turkey breast slices
* 2 tbsp sherry vinegar
* 1 tbsp tomato purée
* 3 stems of fresh thyme, leaves stripped
* little low-fat cooking spray
* salt and pepper

Salsa

* 1 small mango, halved, pitted, peeled and diced
* 1 small red pepper, halved, deseeded and chopped
* 2 spring onions, finely chopped
* finely grated rind of 1 lime and juice of ½ lime

Jerk rub

* 1 tsp ground allspice
* 1 tsp paprika
* 1 tsp dried crushed red chillies
* juice of ½ lime

How to make it

To make the salsa, put the mango, red pepper and spring onions in a bowl, then stir in the lime rind and juice and season with a little salt and pepper.

Put the lettuce in a large shallow bowl, sprinkle with the juice of one lime and a little salt and pepper and toss.

To make the jerk rub, put the allspice, paprika, chillies and a pinch of salt in a bowl. Add the juice of half a lime and mix.

Preheat the grill to hot. Arrange the pineapple in a single layer on a small baking tray and sprinkle with a little of the jerk rub. Grill for 2–3 minutes, until just beginning to brown. Transfer to a plate.

Arrange the turkey slices on the grill rack. Add the sherry vinegar, tomato purée and thyme leaves to the jerk rub, then spread over the turkey. Spray with cooking spray, then grill for 12–15 minutes, turning and brushing with the pan juices once, until browned and cooked through. Cut through the middle of a slice to check that the meat is no longer pink and any juices run clear and are piping hot. Cut into thin strips.

Nestle the warm pineapple in the lettuce leaves, pile the turkey on top, then spoon over the salsa and serve on four plates.

Per serving: 217 cals 2.2g fat 0.5g sat fat 28.3g protein 22g carbs 3.3g fibre

Chicken cobb salad

Per serving: 270 cals   14.6g fat   4.7g sat fat   27g protein   8.2g carbs   4g fibre

A classic salad made low calorie with a lovely and light dressing — perfect for lunch or a starter if you're planning a healthy meal for friends.

Serves 4

* 2 eggs
* little low-fat cooking spray
* 4 rashers of turkey bacon, diced
* 2 cos lettuce, leaves separated and cut into bite-sized pieces
* 200 g/7 oz tomatoes, cut into wedges
* 225 g/8 oz cooked skinless, boneless chicken breast, diced
* 55 g/2 oz blue cheese, crumbled

Dressing

* 2 tbsp balsamic vinegar
* 1 tsp Dijon mustard
* 2 tbsp olive oil
* ¼ tsp salt
* ¼ tsp pepper

It's chicken time!

To make the dressing, put all the ingredients in a bowl and whisk together.

Put the eggs in a saucepan and pour in enough cold water to cover them by 1 cm/½ inch. Bring to the boil, then reduce the heat and simmer for 8 minutes. Drain immediately, cool quickly under cold running water, then peel, discard the yolks and chop the whites.

Place a frying pan sprayed with low-fat cooking spray over a medium—high heat. Add the bacon and cook for 2—3 minutes, or until lightly coloured, crisp and cooked through.

Put the lettuce and tomatoes in a bowl and toss gently together. Drizzle over enough dressing to coat. Divide the salad between four plates and top with the chicken, bacon, cheese and egg whites. Drizzle with the remaining dressing and serve immediately.

Vietnamese shredded chicken salad

Per serving: 267 cals 7g fat 2g sat fat 37g protein 13.8g carbs 3.8g fibre

This salad is dressed with a concentrated homemade chicken stock mixed with zingy lime juice, rather than an oil-based vinaigrette, for a fresh-tasting dish that's low in fat and carbs.

Serves 4

* 2 carrots
* 1 courgette
* 150 g/5½ oz ready-to-eat beansprouts
* 2 Little Gem lettuces, thickly sliced
* 25 g/1 oz fresh coriander, roughly chopped

Chicken

* 1 kg/2 lb 4 oz ready-to-cook whole chicken
* 2 lemon grass stems, halved lengthways
* 1 celery stick, sliced
* 1 onion, quartered
* 2 carrots, sliced
* 1.2 litres/2 pints cold water
* 2 tbsp soy sauce

Dressing

* finely grated rind and juice of ½ lime
* 1 red chilli, deseeded and finely chopped
* 2 tsp fish sauce

Time to get started

To cook the chicken, put it, breast side down, in a deep saucepan only a little bigger than the bird. Add the lemon grass, celery, onion and carrots. Pour in the water, ensuring it covers the bird, and add the soy sauce. Bring to the boil, cover and simmer for 1 hour, or until cooked through. Lift the chicken out of the pan. To check it is cooked, pierce the thickest part of the leg between the drumstick and thigh with a skewer; any juices should be piping hot and clear, with no traces of pink. Cover and leave to cool. Boil the stock for 30—45 minutes, until reduced to 250 ml/9 fl oz. Strain into a gravy separator and leave to cool.

Shave the carrots and courgette into long, thin ribbons using a swivel-bladed vegetable peeler, and put them in a salad bowl. Add the beansprouts, lettuce and coriander and toss together.

To make the dressing, strain the fat off the chicken stock, then measure out 150 ml/5 fl oz of the liquid and pour it into a large bowl. Add the lime rind and juice, chilli and fish sauce and mix.

Take the meat off the chicken, shred it into thin strips (discarding the skin and bones) and add it to the dressing, then toss gently together. Spoon the salad on to four plates, top with the chicken and dressing and serve.

Chicken for calorie counters

Although chicken meat is low in calories, discard the skin if you are watching your calorie intake and skim the fat from homemade stock to keep fat levels low.

Asian tuna & wild rice salad

Per serving: 334 cals 0.8g fat 0.1g sat fat 21g protein 60g carbs 2.9g fibre

This filling rice salad is a healthy mix of high-fibre wild rice, protein-rich tuna and crunchy vegetables, tossed in an oil-free, low-calorie soy and ginger dressing.

Serves 4

* 55 g/2 oz wild rice
* 200 g/7 oz long-grain white rice
* 70 g/2½ oz cucumber, diced
* 85 g/3 oz button mushrooms, quartered
* 25 g/1 oz fresh coriander, roughly chopped
* 200 g/7 oz can tuna in natural spring water, drained and flaked
* 125 g/4½ oz asparagus, trimmed
* 55 g/2 oz mangetout, thinly sliced

Dressing

* finely grated rind and juice of 1 lime
* 2-cm/¾-inch piece of fresh ginger, peeled and finely grated
* 3 tbsp light soy sauce
* 2 tbsp sweet chilli dipping sauce

How to make it

Put the wild rice in a saucepan of boiling water. Bring back to the boil, then simmer, uncovered, for 10 minutes. Add the white rice and cook for 8—10 minutes, or until all the grains are tender. Drain, rinse, drain again, then transfer to a salad bowl.

Add the cucumber, mushrooms and coriander, toss gently together, then scatter over the tuna.

To make the dressing, put all the ingredients in a small bowl. Whisk together until smooth, then drizzle over the salad and toss gently together.

Lay a stem of asparagus on a chopping board, then shave it into long, thin ribbons using a swivel-bladed vegetable peeler. Continue until all the stems have been sliced.

Divide the salad between four plates. Top with the asparagus and mangetout and serve.

Smoked salmon & asparagus salad with crab dressing

Per serving: 135 cals   3.7g fat   0.8g sat fat   19.5g protein   7g carbs   3.4g fibre

This luxurious salad is super-quick to prepare and will leave your friends really impressed! If you can't find fresh or frozen crab in the supermarket, cheat and use canned.

Serves 4

* 300 g/10½ oz asparagus, trimmed
* 1 butterhead lettuce, leaves separated and torn into bite-sized pieces
* 1 red-tinged Little Gem or lollo rosso lettuce, leaves separated and torn into bite-sized pieces
* 200 g/7 oz sliced smoked salmon, cut into strips
* 125 g/4½ oz fresh white cooked crab meat
* pinch of paprika, to garnish

Dressing

* 2 tbsp reduced-fat crème fraîche
* 2 tbsp dark cooked crab meat
* pinch of ground mace (optional)
* juice of 1 lemon
* salt and pepper

Toss it together

Put the asparagus in the top of a steamer, cover and set over a saucepan of simmering water. Steam for 4—5 minutes, or until tender. Leave to cool.

Put all the lettuce leaves in a salad bowl. Top with the smoked salmon, then sprinkle with the white crab meat.

To make the dressing, put the crème fraîche, dark crab meat and mace, if using, in a small bowl. Whisk together until smooth, then gradually mix in the lemon juice and season with a little salt and pepper.

Divide the salad between four plates. Top with the asparagus, then drizzle with the dressing and garnish with the paprika.

Selenium for fertility

Crab and other shellfish are good sources of the trace mineral selenium, which works with vitamin E for normal growth and fertility, good liver function and hormone production. As an antioxidant, it is believed to help offset the effects of oxidized fats, which can contribute to the growth of cancerous tumours.

Super-light salad Niçoise

A classic French salad, made with a reduced-oil dressing to keep the calories down and topped with melt-in-the-mouth slices of griddled fresh tuna and dainty quails' eggs. It's higher in calories than most in this chapter, but filling enough to be a great main course.

Serves 4

* 400 g/14 oz baby new potatoes, thickly sliced
* 150 g/5½ oz broccoli, cut into small florets, stems sliced
* 150 g/5½ oz green beans, halved
* 2 Romaine lettuce hearts, leaves separated and larger ones shredded
* 300 g/10½ oz tomatoes, diced
* 150 g/5½ oz cucumber, halved lengthways, deseeded and diced
* ½ red onion, thinly sliced
* 85 g/3 oz black olives, stoned
* 2 tbsp roughly chopped fresh flat-leaf parsley
* 12 quails' eggs
* 2 x 225 g/8 oz tuna steaks
* little low-fat cooking spray
* salt and pepper

Dressing

* juice of 1 lemon
* 2 tbsp olive oil
* 3 tbsp balsamic vinegar

Create your salad

Put the potatoes in the top of a steamer, cover and set over a saucepan of simmering water. Steam for 6—8 minutes, or until tender. Lift off the steamer and leave to cool. Add the broccoli and beans to the simmering water and cook for 2 minutes, or until just tender, then drain and leave to cool.

To make the dressing, put the lemon juice, oil and vinegar in a jam jar, season with a little salt and pepper, screw on the lid and shake well.

Put the lettuce in a salad bowl, then sprinkle with the tomatoes, cucumber, red onion, olives and parsley. Add the potatoes, broccoli and green beans. Drizzle over the dressing and toss gently together.

Cook the quails' eggs according to the packet instructions. Drain and rinse with cold water. Preheat a ridged griddle pan over a high heat. Spray the tuna with low-fat cooking spray, season with salt and pepper and cook for 1½ minutes on each side for rare or 2½ minutes on each side for medium, using more spray if needed. Cut into thin slices.

Divide the salad between four plates. Peel some of the quails' eggs and leave others with their shells on, then cut them in half. Nestle them in the salads, top with the tuna and serve.

Per serving: 387 cals 13.8g fat 2.6g sat fat 33.7g protein 33.9g carbs 8g fibre

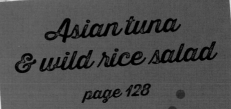

Asian tuna & wild rice salad

page 128

Smoked salmon & asparagus salad with crab dressing

page 129

Prawn taco salad

Per serving: 226 cals 9g fat 1.3g sat fat 19.6g protein 19.5g carbs 5g fibre

Make tortillas go further by cutting them into thin strips and tossing them in your salad. They contrast brilliantly with crisp lettuce leaves and fresh prawns.

Serves 4

* 2 corn tortillas
* little low-fat cooking spray
* 500 g/1 lb 2 oz cos lettuce, chopped
* 300 g/10½ oz cucumber, thinly sliced
* 135 g/4¾ oz frozen sweetcorn kernels, thawed
* 2 tomatoes, cut into half-wedges
* 450 g/1 lb cooked peeled prawns, thawed if frozen

Dressing

* 2 tbsp olive oil
* 2 tbsp lime juice
* 1 garlic clove, finely chopped
* ½ tsp ground cumin
* ½ tsp salt
* 1 tbsp finely chopped red onion
* 1 tbsp finely chopped fresh coriander

Time to get started

Preheat the oven to 200°C/400°F/Gas Mark 6. Line a baking tray with foil.

Spray the tortillas on both sides with low-fat cooking spray. Cut them in half, then cut the halves into 5-mm/¼-inch wide strips. Put the strips on the baking tray in a single layer and bake for 10 minutes, or until crisp and lightly browned. Leave to cool on the tray.

To make the dressing, put the oil, lime juice, garlic, cumin and salt in a bowl and whisk together until emulsified. Stir in the onion and coriander.

Put the lettuce, cucumber, sweetcorn and tomatoes in a salad bowl and toss gently together. Add several spoonfuls of the dressing and toss again. Divide the salad between four plates. Top with the cooked prawns and drizzle with the remaining dressing. Garnish with the tortilla and serve immediately.

Power prawns

Prawns are low in calories and an excellent source of the antioxidant mineral selenium and of the antioxidant and anti-inflammatory nutrient astaxanthin.

Bean salad with feta

Per serving: 249 cals 21g fat 5.1g sat fat 5.1g protein 11.8g carbs 3.6g fibre

A little soft feta goes a long way in this salad, adding salty seasoning to the crunchy beans and radishes and the sweet tomatoes.

Serves 4

* 350 g/12 oz green beans
* 1 red onion, finely chopped
* 3 tbsp finely chopped fresh coriander
* 2 radishes, thinly sliced
* 75 g/2¾ oz feta cheese (drained weight), crumbled
* 1 tsp finely chopped fresh oregano or ½ tsp dried oregano
* 2 tbsp red wine vinegar
* 5 tbsp extra virgin olive oil
* 225 g/8 oz tomatoes, cut into wedges
* pepper

To make this salad

Put the beans in a saucepan of boiling water. Bring back to the boil, then simmer for 5 minutes, or until tender. Drain, rinse with cold water, then drain again. Cut them in half and transfer them to a salad bowl. Add the onion, coriander, radishes and feta.

Sprinkle the oregano over the salad, then season to taste with pepper.

To make the dressing, put the vinegar and oil in a bowl and whisk. Drizzle over the salad, add the tomatoes, toss gently together and serve.

Great green beans

Tender and slender, green beans are a good source of micro-nutrients, minerals and vitamins. Plus they are cholesterol-free, rich in dietary fibre for good colon health and soluble fibre to help slow down the metabolism of carbohydrate, which regulates blood sugar levels.

Vegetable confetti with omelette spirals

Per serving: 378 cals   12.6g fat   3.4g sat fat   16.8g protein   48g carbs   6.6g fibre

For a filling salad that's low in calories, look no further than this colourful treat. The veg all keep well in the fridge, so it's a great stand-by meal for after work.

Serves 4

* 900 ml/1 pint 10 fl oz vegetable stock
* 225 g/8 oz quinoa
* 1 courgette, coarsely grated
* 1 carrot, coarsely grated
* 200 g/7 oz raw beetroots, green stalk trimmed, coarsely grated

Dressing

* finely grated rind and juice of 1 unwaxed lemon
* 2 tbsp light soy sauce
* 25 g/1 oz fresh coriander, finely chopped
* pepper

Omelette

* 4 eggs
* 1 small red chilli, deseeded and finely chopped
* 2 tbsp roughly chopped fresh coriander
* 2 tbsp water
* 2 tsp sunflower oil

For something 'eggstra' special...

Bring the stock to the boil in a saucepan, add the quinoa and simmer for 10—12 minutes, until the germs separate from the seeds. Drain off the stock and discard, and spoon the quinoa into a salad bowl. Leave to cool.

To make the dressing, put the lemon rind and juice and soy sauce in a small bowl and whisk together. Add the coriander, season with a little pepper and stir.

Add the courgette, carrot and beetroot to the quinoa. Drizzle over the dressing and toss gently together.

To make the omelette, crack the eggs into a jug, add the chilli, coriander and water, season with pepper and whisk together. Heat 1 teaspoon of the oil in a frying pan over a medium heat. Pour in half the egg mixture and cook, gently moving the softly set egg in folds towards the centre of the pan, for 4—5 minutes, until the underside is golden and the egg is just set. Loosen the edges, slide the omelette on to a chopping board, roll it up, then leave to cool for 5 minutes. Make a second omelette in the same way. Thinly slice and arrange over the top of the salad.

Carrots

Carrots are rich in beta carotene, which is converted by the body into vitamin A. This nourishes the skin and helps to keep wrinkles at bay. The soluble fibre carrots contain helps lower cholesterol and the carotenoids may lower the risk of heart disease.

Reduced-calorie potato salad

Per serving: 145 cals 0.8g fat 0.4g sat fat 5.1g protein 29g carbs 4.3g fibre

Watching your weight doesn't mean you have to miss out on potato salad. Simply replace calorie-laden mayonnaise with a healthier virtually fat-free yogurt-and-herb dressing.

Serves 4

* 650 g/1 lb 7 oz baby new potatoes, thickly sliced
* 25 g/1 oz rocket

Dressing

* 150 g/5½ oz low-fat natural yogurt
* 1 tsp Dijon mustard
* ½ tsp powdered sweetener
* 2 spring onions, finely chopped
* 4 tbsp roughly chopped fresh dill
* 50 g/1¾ oz fresh flat-leaf parsley, finely chopped
* salt and pepper

Steam power

Bring out the full flavour of new potatoes by steaming them rather than boiling them. Steamed potatoes taste better, and the vitamin C found in the skins is not lost into the cooking water. Potatoes also contain vitamin B and fibre, but are best known as a source of energy-boosting complex carbohydrates. They are low in fat and contain small amounts of protein.

Toss it together

Put the potatoes in the top of a steamer, cover and set over a saucepan of simmering water. Steam for 6—8 minutes, or until tender. Lift off the steamer and leave to cool for 10 minutes.

Meanwhile, to make the dressing, put the yogurt in a large bowl. Add the mustard and sweetener and stir well. Add the spring onions, dill and parsley, season well with salt and pepper and stir again.

Add the warm potatoes to the dressing and toss gently together, then leave to cool completely. Spoon into four bowls, top with the rocket and serve.

Spinach, courgette & mint salad

Per serving: 75 calories   1.3g fat   0.5g sat fat   5.9g protein   11.8g carbs   3.6g fibre

A light, fresh courgette-based salad bathed in a super-healthy, low-fat dressing made with natural yogurt.

Serves 4

* 2 courgettes, cut into batons
* 100 g/3½ oz green beans, cut into thirds
* 1 green pepper, halved, deseeded and cut into strips
* 2 celery sticks, sliced
* 200 g/7 oz baby spinach

Dressing

* 200 g/7 oz low-fat natural yogurt
* 1 garlic clove, finely chopped
* 2 tbsp roughly chopped fresh mint
* pepper

Time to get started

Put the courgettes and beans in a saucepan of boiling water. Bring back to the boil, then simmer for 5 minutes, or until just tender. Drain into a colander, rinse with cold water, then drain again. Transfer to a salad bowl and leave to cool.

Add the green pepper, celery and spinach, tearing any larger leaves into bite-sized pieces.

To make the dressing, put the yogurt, garlic and mint in a bowl. Season to taste with pepper. Drizzle the dressing on to the salad and serve immediately.

Spinach for strength

Just 100 g/3½ oz of spinach per day provides 25 per cent of the iron we need. There's plenty of soluble fibre in it too, as well as vitamins A, B6 and C, potassium, manganese, magnesium, copper and zinc. It's a rich source of omega-3 fatty acids too, making it an all-round nutrition powerhouse!

Broccoli

Health organisations rave about broccoli as a must-have food for two powerful phytochemicals: indoles and the isothiocyanate 'sulforaphane', thought to increase a group of enzymes that help fight cancer-causing agents, particularly in the prostate gland. Broccoli is also a good source of the antioxidant vitamins beta carotene and vitamin C. The darker the florets, the more beta carotene and vitamin C they contain. Steam rather than boil it to retain as much vitamin C as you can. Broccoli contains folic acid, which is essential for mums-to-be, iron and potassium. For those who do not eat dairy, broccoli can be a valuable source of calcium, and the soluble fibre it contains helps draw cholesterol out of your body. So keep on encouraging the family to eat more broccoli!

Green salad with yogurt dressing

Per serving: 122 cals 7.6g fat 1.3g sat fat 3.8g protein 10.7g carbs 2.3g fibre

This colourful green salad is a perfect slimming lunch,
and a great accompaniment for meat or fish.

Serves 4

* 150 g/5½ oz cucumber, thinly sliced
* 6 spring onions, finely chopped
* 150 g/5½ oz tomatoes, sliced
* 1 yellow pepper, halved, deseeded and cut into strips
* 2 celery sticks, thinly sliced
* 4 radishes, thinly sliced
* 85 g/3 oz rocket

Dressing

* 2 tbsp lemon juice
* 1 garlic clove, crushed
* 150 g/5½ oz low-fat natural yogurt
* 2 tbsp olive oil
* salt and pepper

To make this salad

Put the cucumber, spring onions, tomatoes, yellow pepper, celery, radishes and rocket in a salad bowl.

To make the dressing, put the lemon juice, garlic, yogurt and olive oil in a bowl and stir well. Season to taste with salt and pepper.

Drizzle the dressing over the salad and toss gently together, then serve immediately.

Rocket power

Rocket is rich in folic acid and vitamins A and B-complex. It is also a very good source of vitamin K. There are minerals too, including iron, manganese, potassium, calcium and phosphorus.

Three-bean salad

Per serving: 290 cals 16.8g fat 5.8g sat fat 12.3g protein 23.5g carbs 7.2g fibre

A small handful of cashew nuts and a little feta cheese give this filling bean salad crunch and creaminess – delicious!

Serves 4

* 85 g/3 oz mixed salad leaves, such as spinach, rocket and curly endive
* ½ red onion, thinly sliced and halved to make half-moons
* 40 g/1½ oz radishes, thinly sliced
* 100 g/3½ oz cherry tomatoes, halved
* 55 g/2 oz cooked beetroot in natural juices (drained weight), drained and diced
* 25 g/1 oz dried cranberries
* 140 g/5 oz canned cannellini beans, drained and rinsed
* 100 g/3½ oz canned red kidney beans, drained and rinsed
* 150 g/5½ oz canned flageolet beans, drained and rinsed
* 25 g/1 oz roasted cashew nuts
* 115 g/4 oz feta cheese (drained weight), crumbled

Dressing

* 2 tbsp extra virgin olive oil
* ½ tsp Dijon mustard
* 1 tbsp lemon juice
* 1 tbsp roughly chopped fresh coriander
* salt and pepper

To make this salad

Put the salad leaves in a salad bowl. Put the onion, radishes, tomatoes, beetroot, cranberries and all the beans in a separate bowl.

To make the dressing, put the oil, mustard, lemon juice and coriander in a jam jar, season to taste with salt and pepper, screw on the lid and shake well. Drizzle over the bean mixture and toss gently together. Spoon this mixture on to the salad leaves.

Spoon into four bowls, scatter over the nuts and feta and serve.

Go nuts for cashews

Cashew nuts have a lower fat content than most nuts, and most of their fat is unsaturated fatty acids. They have a high antioxidant content, which may be key to their heart-protective benefits.

Mediterranean wrap

Per serving: 298 cals   15.4g fat   2.5g sat fat   7.3g protein   32.3g carbs   4.5g fibre

Perfect for a packed lunch or quick treat,
this salad-in-a-wrap is sure to be popular with all the family.

Serves 4

* 1 small courgette, thickly sliced
* 1 red pepper, halved, deseeded and cut into chunks
* 1 tbsp olive oil
* 4 soft flatbreads
* 6 tbsp sun-dried tomato purée
* 85 g/3 oz baby spinach, shredded
* 4 artichoke hearts in oil, drained and quartered
* 8 sun-dried tomatoes in oil, drained and quartered
* 16 black olives, stoned and halved
* 50 g/1¾ oz fresh basil leaves, torn

Wrap it up

Preheat the oven to 190°C/375°F/Gas Mark 5. Arrange the courgette and pepper on a baking tray in a single layer, pour over the oil and toss together to coat. Roast for 20 minutes, or until softened and beginning to brown.

Meanwhile, spread each flatbread with a thin layer of sun-dried tomato purée, then top with the spinach.

Put the roast vegetables, artichokes, sun-dried tomatoes, olives and basil in a bowl and toss together. Divide the mixture between the flatbreads. Roll the flatbreads up tightly, slice in half and serve.

The art of the artichoke

Globe artichokes are a good source of dietary fibre. They also contain good amounts of folic acid and vitamins B-complex, C and K, and are a source of minerals such as copper, calcium, manganese, phosphorus and iron.

Summer garden salad

Per serving: 124 cals   7.3g fat   0.5g sat fat   5.8g protein   17.8g carbs   8.3g fibre

A spicy, low-fat tomato dressing makes a lovely match for runner beans and crisp lettuce. This salad is great on its own, or served with sliced and barbecued chicken or fish.

Serves 4

* 500 g/1 lb 2 oz runner beans, thinly sliced
* 300 g/10½ oz tomatoes, diced
* 2 Little Gem lettuces, leaves separated
* 25 g/1 oz fresh mint, finely chopped
* 25 g/1 oz fresh chives, roughly snipped

Dressing

* 2 tsp olive oil
* 1 red onion, finely chopped
* 2 garlic cloves, finely chopped
* 500 g/1 lb 2 oz tomatoes, diced
* 1 tsp smoked hot paprika
* 3 tbsp sherry vinegar
* salt and pepper

Mix it up

Put the beans in a saucepan of boiling water. Bring back to the boil, then simmer for 3—4 minutes, or until just tender. Drain into a colander, rinse with cold water, then drain again and leave to cool.

To make the dressing, heat the oil in a saucepan over a medium—low heat. Add the onion and fry for 5 minutes, until just beginning to soften. Add the garlic, tomatoes and paprika, then the vinegar, and season well with salt and pepper. Cover and simmer for 5 minutes, until the tomatoes are softened and saucy. Transfer to a salad bowl and leave to cool.

Add the beans to the dressing and toss gently together. Add the uncooked tomatoes, lettuces, mint and chives, toss gently together, then serve.

Protective tomatoes

Vitamins A, C and E and the minerals zinc and selenium, all found in tomatoes, can help to disarm the free radicals that are produced when the body is under stress. Lycopene, the carotene pigment that turns tomatoes red, may also help to prevent some forms of cancer by lessening the damage caused by free radicals.

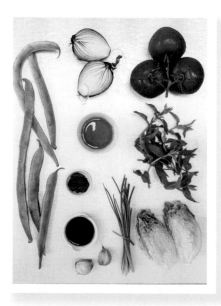

Detox

Red cabbage & baby leaf salad with smoky aubergine dip

Per serving: 315 cals   16.7g fat   1.6g sat fat   7.3g protein   38.6g carbs   13.4g fibre

Give your digestive system a break with this fresh salad. Grilling aubergines until blackened all over gives this dip a wonderfully smoky flavour. Alternatively, they can be barbecued or roasted in a hot oven.

Serves 4

* 2 carrots
* 350 g/12 oz red cabbage, shredded
* 55 g/2 oz raisins
* 125 g/4½ oz bistro salad, a mix of red-stemmed baby red chard, bull's blood chard and lamb's lettuce
* juice of 1 orange
* pepper

Dip

* 3 aubergines
* 3 garlic cloves, finely chopped
* 2 tbsp tahini
* 3 tbsp hemp oil

Time for a dip

To make the dip, preheat the grill to high and remove the grill rack. Prick both ends of each aubergine with a fork, put them in the grill pan and grill 5 cm/2 inches away from the heat source, turning several times, for 15—20 minutes, until blackened. Leave to cool.

Shave the carrots into long, thin ribbons using a swivel-bladed vegetable peeler, then put them on a serving plate. Add the cabbage, then sprinkle over the raisins and salad leaves. Drizzle with the orange juice and season with a little pepper.

Cut the aubergines in half and scoop the soft flesh away from the blackened skins using a dessert spoon. Finely chop the flesh, then put it in a bowl. Add the garlic, tahini and hemp oil, season with a little pepper and mix. Spoon into a serving bowl and nestle in the centre of the salad. Allow diners to spoon the dip over to taste.

Red cabbage for detox

With its intense deep-purple colour, red cabbage has a strong concentration of antioxidants – flavonoids that have been linked to cancer protection and indoles thought to help reduce the risk of breast cancer by altering oestrogen metabolism.

Frisée salad with walnut oil dressing

Per serving: 200 cals 19.3g fat 2.3g sat fat 3g protein 5.7g carbs 2.3g fibre

Going on a detox can mean enjoying much simpler meals, such as this lovely and light, crisp salad with honey-toasted walnuts.

Serves 4

* ½ frisée lettuce, leaves separated and torn into bite-sized pieces
* 1 Romaine lettuce heart, leaves separated and torn into bite-sized pieces

Dressing

* 55 g/2 oz walnut pieces, larger pieces broken up
* 3 tbsp olive oil
* 1 tsp runny honey
* 1 tbsp white wine vinegar
* 1 tsp Dijon mustard
* pepper

Love your lettuce

To make the dressing, put the walnuts in a frying pan, add 1 tablespoon of the oil and cook over a medium heat for 2–3 minutes, or until lightly toasted. Remove from the heat, drizzle over the honey and stir; the heat from the pan will be enough to caramelize the mixture slightly.

Add the remaining oil, stir, then leave to cool for 15 minutes so the walnuts flavour the oil. When it is cool, put the vinegar and mustard in a small bowl, season with a little pepper and beat together, then stir into the walnuts and oil.

Put the frisée and Romaine lettuces in a salad bowl. Spoon over the dressing, toss gently together and serve.

Why eat walnuts?

Walnut oil is composed largely of polyunsaturated fatty acids. They are rich in protein and fibre, and provide many of the essential amino acids.

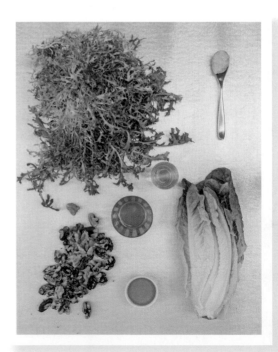

Gado gado salad

Per serving: 255 cals   17.9g fat   2.7g sat fat   10.4g protein   17.5g carbs   6.1g fibre

Tossing raw cauliflower and broccoli with crunchy beansprouts and cucumber and coating them with an Indonesian toasted peanut and soy dressing turns everyday ingredients into something exotic and good for you.

Serves 4

* 250 g/9 oz cauliflower, cored and cut into small florets
* 115 g/4 oz broccoli, destemmed and cut into small florets
* 115 g/4 oz Savoy cabbage, shredded
* 150 g/5½ oz ready-to-eat beansprouts
* 300 g/10½ oz cucumber, peeled, halved lengthways, deseeded and thickly sliced
* 1 red pepper, halved, deseeded and finely chopped

Dressing

* 2 tbsp groundnut oil
* 85 g/3 oz unsalted peanuts, finely chopped
* 2 garlic cloves, finely chopped
* 2 tbsp soy sauce
* juice of 2 limes
* ½ red chilli, deseeded and finely chopped

Toss it together

Put the cauliflower, broccoli, cabbage, beansprouts, cucumber and red pepper in a salad bowl and toss gently together.

To make the dressing, heat 1 tablespoon of the oil in a frying pan over a medium heat. Add the peanuts and garlic and stir-fry for 2–3 minutes, or until lightly browned. Remove from the heat and stir in the soy sauce, lime juice, chilli and remaining oil, then leave to cool.

When ready to eat, spoon the dressing over the salad and toss gently together. Spoon into four bowls, then serve immediately.

Beansprout bonanza

Popular in Chinese and Asian recipes, mung beansprouts are widely available in supermarkets all year round. Low in calories, they can be added to salads in place of noodles or rice.

Rainbow salad with wasabi dressing

Per serving: 117 cals 8.8g fat 0.8g sat fat 4g protein 7.4g carbs 1.7g fibre

A salad doesn't need to be complicated to be good, it just comes down to the quality of the ingredients. This bright, healthy salad is a fun way to encourage children and adults to be more adventurous with the vegetables they eat.

Serves 4

* 1 tbsp sunflower oil
* 4 tbsp sunflower seeds
* 2 tbsp soy sauce
* 200 g/7 oz rainbow chard leaves, shredded and cut into strips

Dressing

* 1 tsp wasabi paste
* 1 tbsp mirin
* juice of 1 small orange
* pepper

How to make it

Heat the oil in a lidded frying pan over a medium heat. Add the sunflower seeds, cover with the lid and fry for 2–3 minutes, shaking the pan so they don't stick, until you hear them begin to pop. Remove the pan from the heat, add the soy sauce, cover with the lid again and leave to cool.

To make the dressing, put the wasabi paste, mirin and orange juice in a jam jar, season with a little pepper, screw on the lid and shake well.

Put the chard leaves in a salad bowl. Drizzle over the dressing then toss gently together. Sprinkle on the toasted sunflower seeds and serve.

Sunflower seeds

Sunflower seeds are a useful source of vitamin E, a powerful antioxidant, and linoleic acid needed for maintenance of cell membranes. You might like to make up extra toasted seeds and store them in a jar in the fridge as a snack.

Buckwheat noodle salad

Per serving: 370 cals   17.5g fat   3.4g sat fat   16g protein   40g carbs   5.9g fibre

A Japanese-inspired salad made with just-cooked soba noodles tossed in a tamari and ginger dressing and speckled with nutrient-boosting broccoli and protein-packed edamame beans.

Serves 4

* 150 g/5½ oz soba noodles
* 200 g/7 oz frozen edamame beans
* 225 g/8 oz broccoli, cut into small florets, stems thinly sliced
* 1 red pepper, halved, deseeded and thinly sliced
* 1 purple or orange pepper, halved, deseeded and thinly sliced
* 115 g/4 oz chestnut mushrooms, thinly sliced
* 85 g/3 oz ready-to-eat sprouting sunflower seeds

Dressing

* 2 tbsp rice vinegar
* 2 tbsp tamari (Japanese soy sauce)
* 4 tbsp rice bran oil
* 4-cm/1½-inch piece of fresh ginger, peeled and finely grated

Full steam ahead

Put cold water in the base of a steamer, bring to the boil, then add the noodles and frozen edamame beans and bring back to the boil. Put the broccoli in the top of the steamer, then put it on the steamer base, cover and steam for 3—5 minutes, or until the noodles and vegetables are just tender. Drain and rinse the noodles and edamame beans, then drain again and tip into a salad bowl. Add the broccoli, then leave to cool.

To make the dressing, put the vinegar, tamari, oil and ginger in a jam jar, screw on the lid and shake well. Drizzle over the salad and toss gently together.

Add the red and purple peppers and mushrooms to the salad and toss again. Spoon into four bowls, then top with the sprouting seeds and serve immediately.

Edamame beans

Japanese edamame or fresh soya beans are a good source of all the essential amino acids, making them an excellent bean to eat if following a vegetarian diet. They are also a good source of the micronutrients, vitamin K, folate, manganese and fibre. It is thought that the isoflavones they contain may mimic the female hormone oestrogen, so helping with symptoms of the menopause.

Miso & tofu salad

Per serving: 204 cals 11.5g fat 1.3g sat fat 12.8g protein 14.5g carbs 4.6g fibre

Protein-rich tofu cooked in a soy, miso and garlic glaze and served with a crisp, crunchy asparagus and beansprout salad – super healthy and super lovely!

Serves 4

* 400 g/14 oz firm tofu, drained and cut into 1-cm/½-inch slices
* 1 tbsp sesame seeds
* 85 g/3 oz mangetout, thinly sliced
* 115 g/4 oz ready-to-eat beansprouts
* 150 g/5½ oz asparagus, trimmed and cut into long, thin slices
* 1 courgette, cut into matchsticks
* 1 Little Gem lettuce, leaves separated and cut into long slices
* 25 g/1 oz fresh coriander, roughly chopped
* 85 g/3 oz mixed ready-to-eat sprouting seeds, such as alfalfa and radish sprouts

Dressing

* 3 tbsp rice wine vinegar
* 2 tbsp soy sauce
* 3 tbsp sunflower oil
* 1 tbsp sweet white miso
* 2 garlic cloves, finely chopped

How to make it

To make the dressing, put the vinegar and soy sauce in a jam jar, then add the oil, miso and garlic. Screw on the lid and shake well.

Preheat the grill to high and line the grill pan with foil. Put the tofu on the foil in a single layer. Mark criss-cross lines over each slice using a knife, then sprinkle with the sesame seeds. Spoon over half the dressing, then grill for 8—10 minutes, turning once, until browned.

Put the mangetout, beansprouts, asparagus, courgette and lettuce on a platter. Pour over the remaining dressing and toss gently together. Sprinkle over the coriander and sprouts, then top with the hot tofu, drizzle with any pan juices and serve immediately.

Quinoa salad with fennel & orange

Per serving: 388 cals 8.3g fat 1.9g sat fat 10g protein 54g carbs 8.4g fibre

Fennel is known to be an effective diuretic and has a calming effect on the stomach, so is a useful addition to any detox diet. It also contains beta carotene and folate.

Serves 4

* 900 ml/1½ pints vegetable stock
* 225 g/8 oz quinoa, rinsed and drained
* 3 oranges
* 250 g/9 oz fennel bulbs, thinly sliced using a mandolin, green feathery tops reserved and torn into small pieces
* 2 spring onions, finely chopped
* 15 g/½ oz fresh flat-leaf parsley, roughly chopped

Dressing

* juice of ½ lemon
* 3 tbsp olive oil
* pepper

How to make it

Bring the stock to the boil in a saucepan, add the quinoa and simmer for 10—12 minutes, or until the germs separate from the seeds. Drain off the stock and discard, then spoon the quinoa into a salad bowl and leave to cool.

Grate the rind from two of the oranges and put it in a jam jar. Cut a slice off the top and bottom of each of the three oranges, then remove the peel in thin vertical slices and discard. Cut between the membranes to remove the orange segments, then squeeze the juice from the membranes into the jam jar.

Add the orange segments, fennel slices, spring onions and parsley to the quinoa.

To make the dressing, add the lemon juice and oil to the jam jar, season to taste with pepper, screw on the lid and shake well. Drizzle over the salad and toss together. Garnish with the fennel fronds and serve immediately.

Get in the queue for quinoa

Quinoa, pronounced 'keen-wa', contains all eight essential amino acids, plus it's cholesterol-free, rich in fibre and minerals and lower in carbs than most grains. It makes a great salad base.

Oat tabbouleh

Per serving: 348 cals   18.2g fat   3.2g sat fat   10.2g protein   37g carbs   7.4g fibre

We tend to think of oats as being just for porridge or flapjacks, but if you buy wholegrain oats, often called 'oat groats', they make a delicious, nutty-tasting salad base that is packed with energy-boosting complex carbs and fibre.

Serves 4

* 1.2 litres/2 pints vegetable stock
* 175 g/6 oz oat groats
* 4 spring onions
* 300 g/10½ oz asparagus
* 1 courgette, diagonally sliced
* 25 g/1 oz fresh mint, roughly chopped

Dressing

* grated rind and juice of 1 unwaxed lemon
* 1 tbsp hemp oil
* 3 tbsp olive oil
* 1 tsp cumin seeds, finely crushed
* 1 tsp coriander seeds, finely crushed
* pepper

How to make it

Pour the stock into a saucepan, bring to the boil, then add the oats. Simmer for 25 minutes, or until the oats are tender and the grains have split. Drain off the stock through a sieve and discard, then spoon the oats into a salad bowl and leave to cool.

To make the dressing, put the lemon rind and juice, hemp oil, olive oil, cumin seeds and coriander seeds in a jam jar, season with a little pepper, screw on the lid and shake well.

Preheat a griddle pan over a high heat. Put the onions, asparagus and courgette in a bowl, drizzle over half the dressing and toss together. Cook in the hot pan for 2—3 minutes, or until just softened and beginning to char, turning from time to time. Leave to cool, then transfer to a clean chopping board and cut into bite-sized pieces.

Add the remaining dressing to the oats and stir. Add the cooled vegetables, sprinkle with the mint and toss gently together. Spoon into four shallow bowls to serve.

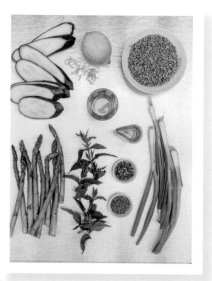

Amazing asparagus

In traditional folk medicine, asparagus was used as a tonic and sedative. We know it best for its antioxidant properties; it is rich in beta carotenes and B group vitamins, plus vitamins C and E. It is not suitable for those who suffer with gout, as it is one of the few vegetables high in purines.

Barley & crushed bean salad

Per serving: 265 cals 15.7g fat 3.3g sat fat 7g protein 22.7g carbs 5.9g fibre

Tossed with summery vegetables, pearl barley makes a filling salad. It's packed with complex carbs and soluble fibre and is a low-GI food.

Serves 4

* 1.2 litres/2 pints vegetable stock
* 150 g/5½ oz pearl barley
* 425 g/15 oz broad beans, podded (175 g/6 oz podded weight)
* 150 g/5½ oz peas
* 2 spring onions, quartered
* 2 stems of fresh tarragon, finely chopped
* 25 g/1 oz fresh flat-leaf parsley, finely chopped
* 25 g/1 oz pea shoots

Dressing

* 2 tbsp flaxseed (linseed) oil
* 2 tbsp rice bran oil
* 1 tbsp white wine vinegar
* 1 tsp Dijon mustard
* 1 tsp coriander seeds, roughly crushed
* ¼ tsp crushed dried red chillies
* pepper

Full of beans...

Put the stock in the base of a steamer, bring to the boil, then add the pearl barley, cover and simmer for 20 minutes. Put the broad beans in the top of the steamer, then put it on the steamer base, cover and steam for 5—10 minutes, or until the barley and beans are just tender.

Drain off the stock and discard, then spoon the barley into a salad bowl. Add one-third of the broad beans and raw peas. Put the remaining broad beans and peas, the spring onions, tarragon and parsley in a food processor and process until finely chopped. Add to the salad bowl.

To make the dressing, put the flaxseed oil, rice bran oil, vinegar, mustard, coriander seeds and chillies in a jam jar, season with pepper, screw on the lid and shake well. Drizzle over the salad and toss gently together, then spoon into four bowls, top with the pea shoots and serve.

Protein boosters

Proteins are an essential constituent of virtually every cell in the body; in fact the word comes from the Greek meaning 'of prime importance'. They are needed for growth and repair of body tissues, to make up enzymes and hormones and as neurotransmitters. Unlike meat, most vegetable proteins do not contain all eight essential amino acids, so aim to mix different vegetable proteins together in one meal by serving grains and pulses together.

Puy lentil & Mediterranean roast vegetable salad

Per serving: 464 cals 21.8g fat 2.4g sat fat 17.8g protein 50g carbs 17g fibre

Lentils and whole grains are vital in any detox diet. Rich in complex carbs, fibre, protein, vitamins and minerals, they make an inexpensive and filling base to any meal. Puy lentils, unlike most pulses, don't need soaking before cooking.

Serves 4

* 2 small red peppers, quartered and deseeded
* 2 courgettes, thickly sliced
* 2 red onions, each cut into 8 wedges
* 400 g/14 oz tomatoes, halved
* 300 g/10½ oz baby aubergines, halved lengthways
* 3 stems of fresh thyme, leaves picked
* 2 garlic cloves, finely chopped
* 3 tbsp olive oil
* 225 g/8 oz puy lentils
* 25 g/1 oz fresh flat-leaf parsley, roughly chopped
* pepper

Dressing

* 3 tbsp hemp oil
* 2 tbsp balsamic vinegar
* juice of 1 lemon

Time to get started

Preheat the oven to 200°C/400°F/Gas Mark 6. Arrange the peppers, skin side up, in a large roasting tin. Add the courgettes, onions, tomatoes and aubergines and arrange in a single layer.

Sprinkle the thyme and garlic over the vegetables. Season with a little pepper and drizzle over the olive oil. Roast for 30 minutes, or until the vegetables are softened and browned around the edges.

Put the lentils in a saucepan of boiling water. Bring back to the boil, then simmer for 20 minutes, or until just tender. Drain into a sieve, rinse with cold water, then drain again. Transfer to a salad bowl and leave to cool.

To make the dressing, put the hemp oil, balsamic vinegar and lemon juice in a jam jar, season with pepper, screw on the lid and shake well.

Drizzle the dressing over the lentils and toss gently together. Peel the skins away from the peppers and cut into slices, then add them to the salad. Add the remaining roast vegetables and any pan juices, then sprinkle with the parsley and serve.

Cutting down on salt

When on a detox, you should try to avoid, or at the very least cut right down on, salt. Too much salt can contribute to high blood pressure, which in turn can lead to heart disease, stroke and kidney problems. We should only consume 6 g, or around 1 tsp, of salt per day. Many processed foods contain more salt than you would imagine. Take the salt pot off the table and try to gradually cut down on the amount you use when cooking. Add spices, herbs, garlic and vinegars as flavourings instead.

Gazpacho salad

Per serving: 140 cals   10.6g fat   1.3g sat fat   2.2g protein   10g carbs   2.5g fibre

All the flavours of this favourite Spanish soup, but in a crunchy nutrient-boosting salad, tossed in a sun-dried tomato dressing.

Serves 4

* 500 g/1 lb 2 oz tomatoes, halved, deseeded and diced
* 85 g/3 oz cucumber, quartered lengthways, deseeded and thickly sliced
* 1 celery stick, diced
* 1 spring onion, finely chopped
* ½ yellow pepper, deseeded and diced
* little fresh basil, to garnish

Dressing

* 40 g/1½ oz sun-dried tomatoes in oil, drained
* 2 tbsp olive oil
* 1 tbsp hemp oil
* 2 tbsp red wine vinegar
* 1 garlic clove, finely chopped
* pinch of dried crushed red chillies
* pepper

How to make it

Put the tomatoes, cucumber, celery and spring onion in a salad bowl, then add the yellow pepper and toss gently together.

To make the dressing, put the sun-dried tomatoes in a blender. Add the olive and hemp oils, then the vinegar, garlic and chillies. Season to taste with pepper, then process until you have a coarse paste.

Spoon the dressing over the salad, toss gently together, then garnish with the basil leaves.

Index